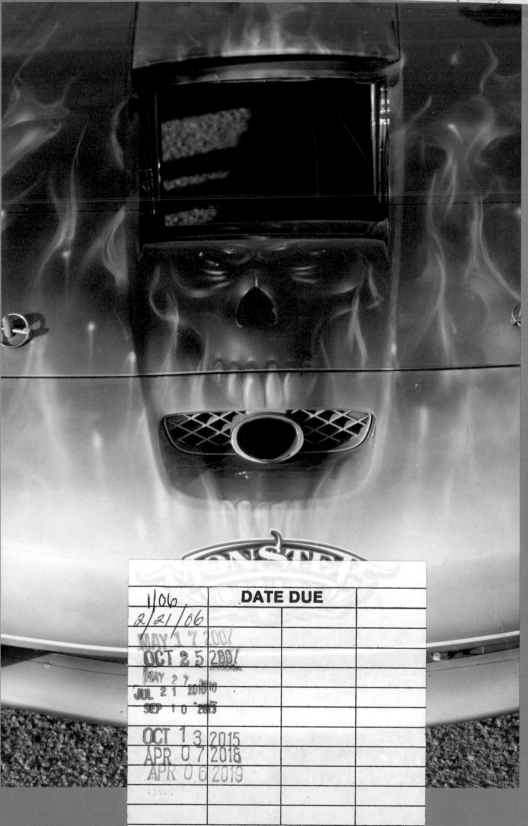

HOW TO
CUSTOM
PAINT
DAMN NEAR ANYTHING

Discovery CHANNEL

entertain your brain™

MOTORBOOKS

This edition first published in 2004 by Motorbooks, an imprint of MBI Publishing Company, Galtier Plaza, Suite 200, 380 Jackson Street, St. Paul, MN 55101-3885 USA

19.95 1/06 Ingram 26879

Motorbooks titles are also available at discounts in bulk quantity for industrial or sales-promotional use. For details write to Special Sales Manager at MBI Publishing Company, Galtier Plaza, Suite 200, 380 Jackson Street, St. Paul, MN 55101-3885 USA.

ISBN 0-7603-1809-3

On the frontispiece: The flamed hood from the Celica Jet Car from Episode 36. The Toyota was powered by a Rolls-Royce Viper MK22 acquired from a two-seat British military trainer. *Discovery Channel*

On the title page: This 1984 Porsche 944 became a golf ball collector in Episode 6. *Discovery Channel*

On the back cover: A 1987 Winnebago was sacrificed to become a mobile skate park for Tony Hawk and Rick Thorne in Episode 18. The clown paint scheme was designed and applied by James Real and Ken Cassidy. *Discovery Channel*

Discovery Communications/Monster Garage book development team:

Thom Beers, Executive Producer, Original Productions

W. Clark Bunting II, Executive Vice President, Discovery Networks U.S.

Sharon M. Bennett, Senior Vice President, Strategic Partnerships & Licensing

Deidre Scott, Vice President, Licensing

Carol Le Blanc, Vice President of Marketing and Retail Development

Sean Gallagher, Director of Programming Development, Discovery Channel

Jeannine Gaubert, Graphic Designer, Licensing

Erica Jacobs Green, Director of Publishing

Acquisitions Editor: Lee Klancher

Associate Editor: Leah Noel

Art directed by Rochelle L. Schultz

Designed by Brenda C. Canales

CONTENTS

The hands-on heroes on *Monster Garage* transform mundane vehicles into fantastic machines. *Discovery Channel*

In the world presented on the Discovery Channel series *Monster Garage*, everyday vehicles are transformed into fantastic creations. Inspired by producer Thom Beers' dreams, the show has struck a resonant chord with America.

The positive response to *Monster Garage* is not difficult to fathom. The heroes of the show are craftspeople, men and women who use their hands to weld, wire, and machine. In one week, the monstrous perform mundane tasks and the mundane become monstrous—Top Fuel dragsters become hot dog machines or Ford Explorers become garbage trucks.

"Live to paint, paint to live."
—Craig Fraser, author and painter

These transformations feed our nation's need for originality in an increasingly homogenous culture. They tap into a cultural hunger for things and thinking that step outside of a top-40, chain-restaurant subdivision reality. The next step for satiating that appetite requires more than watching a television show. We need to get our hands dirty.

One way to do that is by customizing. Put a little monster into our own mundane machines. You can do this with off-the-shelf accessories, something people

are doing at unprecedented rates. Sales of custom wheels are rapidly growing, and interest in automotive aftermarket equipment is at an all-time high.

Bolt-on parts add to your vehicle's look and allow you to personalize a mass-produced machine. But they are still parts that anyone with money and the inclination can find. Custom paint is even more unique and personal, and after acquiring relatively simple materials and equipment, you can experiment with it in your garage.

Painting is a primal experience. Most of us start doing it as kids, with our hands covered in finger paint, creating smears of color roughly resembling trees, houses, and parents. The experience was a joy for most, and yet most of us stopped due to a lack of talent, drive, or time. Well, you can pick up again. You may even find yourself pinstriping your car, or at least your toaster.

Inside this book, you'll find tips and techniques from some of the most innovative professionals in the industry, from the Monster Garage paint team to Von Franco and Enamel to Jon Kosmoski and Jack Giachino.

So in this world of prepackaged food, cookie-cutter houses, and mind-numbing jobs and TPS reports, some old-fashioned handcrafting is more than a hobby or a luxury: it's a great escape. Plus you can make your car, motorcycle, or toaster look really cool. What do you have to lose?

the

PLAN ™

PART 1

VISION

BY TIM REMUS

Planning for a new custom paint job is the most important step in the whole project. Ordering paint, doing bodywork, applying graphics and pinstripes—all those steps might be more exciting, but the task of deciding on a vision and then choosing appropriate colors and paint schemes is the most important part of the process.

At most professional shops and even on the set of *Monster Garage*, the planning comes before anything else. You need to know not only the budget, you also need to have a vision. The nostalgia trend is in full swing; anyone trying to build a car that looks like it came from another era needs to lock in that era and get all the details just right. Today's custom car world encompasses a wide variety of car types and styles. The good news is that you can build pretty much anything you want to and, with good execution, come out with a custom that turns heads down at the local drive-in. The bad news is that it can be hard to pick exactly what you want from such a vast menu.

Many professional shops use a rendering or formal drawing to cement the concept for the car. If customers do not have an exact idea of what they want, a designer like Thom Taylor or Chip Foose is hired to work through a series of sketches until the customer says, "That's it, that's the car." Then the sketch is used to make a full rendering, complete with paint color and graphics.

Start your plan for the new custom by clipping magazine photos of your favorite customs, or build a photo file of machines with the look you're after. You don't have to build a clone of what you see at a show, but if something has the "look" you're trying to achieve, it makes sense to define and use the essential parts of that look.

During the early part of this process, pay attention to things like the body proportions of the vehicles you study. Note the rake, whether the top is chopped, the tire sizes front and back . . . these are all critical dimensions. As one experienced builder explained, "What's important is the proportions of the car, not just the dimensions."

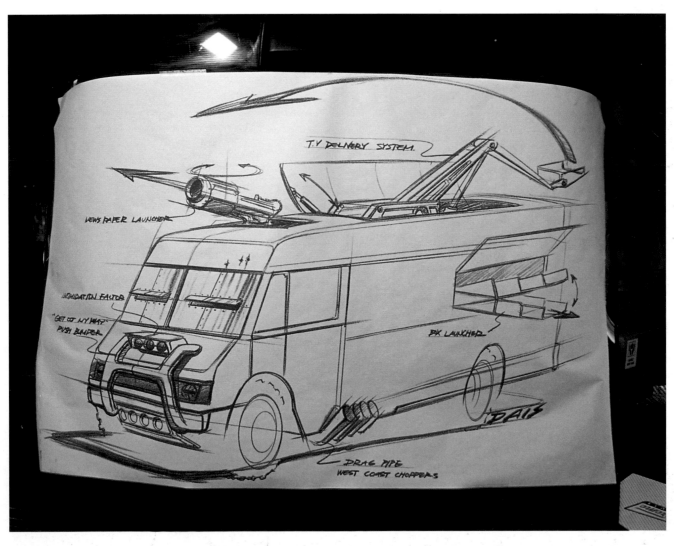

As with a custom vehicle or a monster machine, the key to making your vision turn out as you hope is planning. *Discovery Channel*

In other words, you need to pay attention to the relationships between the parts of the car. How much you chop a top has a major impact on the car's looks, partly for some not-so-obvious reasons. The relationship between the height of the top and the mass of the body is terribly important and helps define the look of the car. When you chop the top, or section or channel a body, you've made a big change in this essential relationship. This is your car—you can do anything you like. Just be sure to think first and paint second.

DESIGN LIKE A PRO

Plenty of hot rodders and custom car builders sketch their projects before starting. Some of those sketches are nothing more than doodles on a napkin. To formalize the process and make it a better prediction of what the new car will really look like, you can borrow some ideas used by professional designers and car builders.

First, start out with a stock side view of the car. This can be a photograph or an image clipped from a magazine. The important thing in either case is that it be a straight side view, without any distortion. Now take the image over to the copy machine and make some big blowups and a whole series of copies.

Next comes the fun part. Using scissors, tape, and anything else you need, add graphics, paint, and other modifications to your heart's content. Study the effect of a variety of treatments. This method will also help you predict how wild you want to go with the look, and how much that might cost.

When you've got the look you want, make some enlargements of the finished product and hang them on the refrigerator. Then check and see how they look in a week.

For the more computer literate among us, a scanner and PC can make the whole process easier. Scan the original into the computer, make some copies of the resulting file, then use a software package like Adobe Photoshop to change the graphics and paint. This might be your opportunity to finally learn how to use the PC you bought the kids for Christmas. Who knows? This could turn into a family project.

The methods don't really matter. What does matter is the end product. Just like the big shops, you want an image of the finished car—one big enough that you can stand back and appreciate its proportions and overall look.

This 1970 Ford Ranchero was transformed into a hydraulically operated bucking bronco dubbed the Low Bull Rider. The paint is one of the nicer schemes on the show. *Discovery Channel*

This Champ Car was used to paint stripes at high speed. The paint was applied by Monster Garage painting guru Tom Prewitt. *Discovery Channel*

This image will be the visual blueprint for the project. It will help keep you excited about the car when energy or money run low and it becomes hard to stay involved. The image taped to the refrigerator or toolbox will also help keep you focused.

CONCRETE PLANNING

You need to know more than just what the car will look like. Obviously, you need to know how much the car will cost as well. Figuring out the true cost means being brutally honest about how much of the car you can paint yourself.

We all have to farm out some of the work. Only a small percentage of us are qualified to do finish paint work. Part of the budgeting process involves breaking the assembly of the car down into various subunits for paint and graphics.

Who isn't a big believer in "do it yourself," whether it's a plumbing project in the house or installing ball joints in the daily driver? In the real world, though, most of us run out of time. The classifieds are always filled with project cars and street rods that didn't get finished. Those projects started off as someone's dream, but somewhere along the line they turned into nightmares. The idea is to finish the car, and to do that you need a certain momentum. Something has to get done every month—preferably every week. By farming out some of the jobs you could do yourself, more total

A subtle set of flames like these on this ambulance can add flash to an otherwise pedestrian vehicle. *Discovery Channel*

Less-subtle flames can also add a great look. *Discovery Channel*

work gets done during a given period, and the slow progress of turning a sketch on the wall into a finished vehicle is more likely to stay on track.

At one shop in southern California they use elaborate planning forms that list every part on the car, along with the price. In fact, the chassis builder's checklist is available on this shop's Web site. Another series of forms lists outside labor for things like sandblasting, polishing, upholstery, paint, chrome, glass cutting and installation, and even the final detailing. Before the project starts, they know exactly how much it's going to cost, how many hours of labor are involved, and how many of the operations will have to be performed by outside shops.

In the same way, you can make a list of all the parts, their cost, and the necessary labor. Now break out the labor you can't or won't do yourself, and get cost estimates. The planning should include time estimates as well.

IT'S GOTTA BE REAL

The planning and estimating needs to be realistic. If you underestimate either the time or money, it's easy to get disappointed when things take longer or cost more than expected. Cost overruns can also play havoc with the family budget and destroy family support for the new hot rod.

Because the finish bodywork and paint are such a big part of the project in terms of both time and money, some home builders finish everything but the body, assemble the car, and drive it in primer for one year. This strategy does stretch out the time needed to truly finish the car, but it puts it on the road that much sooner.

The biggest advantage to this method is that you can go out and have fun with the car now, instead of

Over-the-top customs like this hearse will require lots of thought and time. And you may need a graveyard as a backdrop for the photograph! *Discovery Channel*

one year from now. Back-to-basics hot rods always have a certain allure and seem to get more popular as time goes on. You don't have to tell them it's unfinished. Just paint it primer black (or gray) and drive it proudly to the local or national event. It also gives you a chance to "debug" the car easily—disassembling an unpainted car for repairs or adjustments is easier and less stressful.

The other advantage of this program is that you allow the bank account to recover while driving the car in primer. When it comes time to pull the body off for that high-quality paint job, you can have the money already set aside in the savings account.

CHAPTER 2.1
paint your MONSTER

BY DENNIS PARKS

With the automotive paint products now available, you have perhaps the best opportunity ever to achieve a perfect paint job. What you must realize before you start is that there's much more to painting a car than squeezing the trigger on a spray gun.

Get the body as straight and as smooth as possible. Painting over imperfections is only going to highlight them. Follow the guidelines in this chapter for

making the surface perfectly paint-ready. You must also mix primers, hardeners, topcoats, and catalysts as directed. The directions are included with the product . . . you just have to read them. The chemistry of automotive paint has already been determined for you. There's no reason to try to "improve" the characteristics of any paint product. Mix the components as directed, apply them as directed, allow them to dry as directed before applying successive coats, and you can create a professional paint job on your car.

You must also have the right tools and, as with most jobs, that also requires the correct safety equipment. Today's paint products are safe to use, but only when used properly. Correct safety equipment, such as respirators, rubber gloves, and painter's coveralls, is essential. Learn what safety equipment is required for each type of paint product.

AUTOMOTIVE PAINTING DEFINED

Depending on the job at hand, paint can be applied to automobile bodies in more than one way. Initially, our cars or trucks roll off the assembly line with a fresh coat of paint. Eventually, they begin to need slight touchups to keep nicks or scratches from blemishing their fresh appearance. This is usually done with a small brush attached to the cap of a bottle of touchup paint. If wear and tear necessitates the painting of small body items or trim, you might use a spray can to bring that finish up to snuff. If your automobile has sustained collision damage, repair will usually involve repainting the affected panel(s) or sections with conventional paint spray guns.

The techniques used to apply automotive paint are determined by the type (and amount) of coverage needed and the condition of the existing surface material. You wouldn't use a full-size spray gun to touch up a small scratch; nor would you expect to use a touchup brush to refinish an entire panel. Likewise, paint from a spray can might be "close enough" in color match and texture to refinish or modify a trim panel, such as a grille or body molding. If the entire vehicle is going to be repainted, however, paint specifically meant for automotive refinishing should be used.

To achieve a visually acceptable, compatible, and durable paint job, use products designed to suit the existing paint finishes or undercoat preparations. The finest paint job in the world will not last if the various layers of body filler, primer, sealers, and final topcoat are not compatible. Simply put, don't try to be a chemist when it comes to repainting your car.

DETERMINING THE TYPE OF PAINT ON YOUR CAR

Before the advent of high-tech polyurethane paint products, cars were painted with either enamel or lacquer products. Each had its own distinct

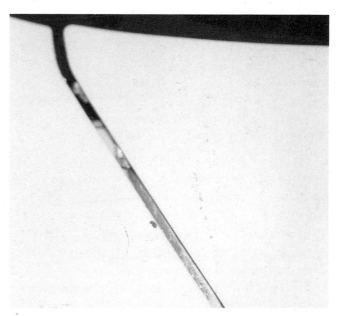

Difficult to see in the photo but readily apparent to the owner of this Oldsmobile is a small scratch on the top edge of the right front fender. About 1/8 inch wide and 3/8 inch long, it's typical of the kind of blemish that can easily be remedied with some touchup paint.

A small scratch on the sheet metal or the edges of this nameplate is the type of damage touchup paint is designed for. The small brush in the cap of a typical touchup bottle would work well to refinish this emblem, whether you remove the emblem or not. If you had some bulk paint designed to be sprayed, you could pour some into a small container and use a fine artist's paintbrush to touch up the emblem.

On the other hand, this rearview mirror is better suited to a spray can of touchup paint. It would be better to remove the mirror to avoid a substantial masking job. Sanding the surface with 400-grit sandpaper, cleaning it with wax and grease remover, then spraying on a couple of thin coats of touchup would work wonders.

characteristics. Enamels were quick and easy, generally covering in one or two coats and not requiring any clearcoats or rubbing out. Lacquer, on the other hand, required multiple coats but allowed imperfections to be easily rubbed out and quickly repainted. Its fast drying time afforded painters the opportunity to fix blemishes almost immediately.

Although both paint products offer benefits, they cannot be used together on car bodies because they're not compatible. It would be all right, under proper conditions, to spray enamel over lacquer when surfaces are properly prepared, but lacquer applied over enamel will almost always result in wrinkling or other severe finish damage. This is because the solvent base for lacquer paint (lacquer thinner) is much too potent for the rather soft materials used in enamel products.

Product compatibility factors are also extremely important today. This is not confined to just enamel, lacquer, or urethane bases. Every product in an entire paint system must be compatible with the surface material to which it will be applied as well as with every other product in the system. For example, using a PPG reducer with a BASF hardener in a DuPont paint product is asking for trouble. The individual products were not designed as parts of a single, compatible paint system, and as a result, the color, adhesion, and surface flow of that combination could be adversely affected.

Before arbitrarily purchasing paint for your car, you need to determine what type of material currently exists on the vehicle's surface: enamel, lacquer, or urethane. On newer vehicles, factory paint jobs are all going to be urethane based, as enamels and lacquers are quickly becoming history. For your vehicle, it's worth asking your local paint supply jobber for information on what kind of paint was applied at the factory. For cars still clad in factory paint jobs, paint codes are listed on their identification tags. In addition, auto body paint and supply store jobbers can determine the type of paint and color from the vehicle identification number (VIN) on older vehicles or from a separate paint and options tag on newer vehicles. This makes material identification easy when you plan to match existing paint.

If your car or truck has been repainted with a type of paint or color different from its original factory job, you'll have to obtain paint code numbers from a paint can used during the repaint or from some other source, such as the painter who completed the job. With luck, that person kept track of this information and will make it available to you.

Should you not be able to determine paint codes or information relating to the type of paint used on your car, you'll have to test an inconspicuous spot on the vehicle body with lacquer thinner. You could also test a spot on an area already slated for repaint. Dab a clean, white cloth with lacquer thinner and rub a spot of paint. If color comes off immediately or the spot begins to wrinkle, the paint type is enamel. Should color wipe off onto the cloth after vigorous rubbing, lacquer paint is present. If nothing wipes off, the paint is probably a type of urethane.

To determine if finishes include coats of clear paint over their base color, sand an inconspicuous spot with 600-grit or finer sandpaper. White sanding residue indicates a clearcoat finish, whereas a color residue demonstrates that the body was painted with a color material only.

I can't place enough emphasis on the importance of determining the type of paint currently covering the surface of your car before you apply new coats of fresh paint. About the only exceptions would be vehicle bodies that have been stripped to bare metal in preparation for complete new paint system applications. If you're still unsure about the type of paint on your car after this test, or if you have any other related questions or problems, consult a professional auto body paint and supply store jobber. Be up front and attentive with that person to receive definitive answers and patient assistance. Remember, applying mismatched coatings to an existing finish can ruin the whole paint job.

NICK AND SCRATCH REPAIR

No matter how hard you try to guard against them, small nicks or paint chips find their way onto new paint finishes much sooner than expected. For vehicles driven on a daily basis, this dilemma is simply unavoidable. Along with rock chips that occur in traffic, parking lot door-slammers are merciless. Add to that a long list of other accidental and careless

Whenever you use spray paint, touchup or otherwise, the spray can should be warm for best results. This will help thoroughly mix the ingredients of the paint and will give the propellant its maximum power. If you need to warm the spray paint, allow it to sit in a sink of warm water before use. Make sure you don't heat spray cans over their recommended safety temperature, which is clearly indicated on the label. Never hold the can over a flame!

This late-model Ford pickup truck is in for a total repaint. All trim, lights, door handles, bumpers, and virtually anything else that can be removed will be, rather than masked. Something to remember with pickup trucks is that for a complete paint job, the bed needs to be removed. This one will be before all of the prep work is completed.

This Dodge sedan suffered some minor damage to the driver's-side doors and rear quarter panel. None of the damage was severe, and almost all of it could be repaired by the hobbyist. Careful attention to detail during the body repair and prep work will go a long way toward making this sedan look like new, once the repairs are completed.

The VIN tag on this pickup truck gives a code that can be deciphered by an auto paint jobber to provide the correct color of paint. Before mixing the paint, it would be a good idea to confirm that the new paint is going to be blue (in this case), just to verify that the vehicle hasn't been repainted or mistagged.

mishaps and, sooner or later, your new paint job will suffer some degree of minor damage. Fortunately, you can repair small nicks with minimal work, provided they're small and the affected paint job is not exotic. You'll need some touchup paint, a small artist's or lettering paintbrush, and masking tape.

Small bottles of stock factory colors of touchup paint are commonly available at auto body paint and supply stores and a number of auto parts houses. Mostly supplied for newer cars, these touchup paints match the paint code on your vehicle's ID tag. They're applied using a small brush attached to the bottle's cap or with an artist's fine paintbrush. For years, auto enthusiasts have successfully used the clean end of paper matchsticks to apply touchup paint.

Clean the damaged area with wax and grease remover and then closely mask off the nick or nicks. Stir or shake the touchup paint as needed. Now, simply dab your paintbrush into the paint and retrieve a small amount of paint on the tip of the bristles. Apply that drop of paint to the nick. Don't attempt to fill in the entire nick depth with the first paint dab. Wait for a while to let the first dab set up, then apply a second small dab.

Continue the dabbing and setting up until paint has filled the nick to just over the surface. It should be obvious before you quit that you've applied touchup paint above the height of the main finish—in other words, it should look as if you put on too much paint. Then let the new paint cure. Don't touch it for a week to 10 days.

After this drying period, mask the nick again. This time, mask a wider area. Then use 1200-grit sandpaper with water to gently smooth the nick area and bring the surface of the new paint down to the surrounding finish. The masking tape will prevent unnecessary sanding on the surface surrounding the repair area.

When you've smoothed the newly applied dabs of paint to the same level as the rest of the finish, remove the masking tape. Then use polish to further blend the repair into its surroundings. If polishing scratches appear, graduate to a finer polish. Let the repair cure for a few weeks before waxing.

Minor nicks and scratches can sometimes be polished or buffed out. They must be shallow and expose only paint at their deepest point. If primer or bare metal is visible, apply new paint.

It's imperative to cover nicks as soon as possible, especially when bare metal is exposed. Oxidation quickly attacks bare metal, beginning a rust and corrosion process. Like a cancer, oxidation spreads undetected beneath paint, until damage is so extensive that flakes of paint peel off at random. Prior to the advent of convenient touchup paint bottles, auto enthusiasts applied dabs of clear fingernail polish to nicks in efforts to protect bare metal and deter the progress of oxidation, rust, and corrosion.

Compared to tiny nicks, long, deep scratches may pose more serious problems. Although minor scratches may be touched up in basically the same fashion as nicks, long strokes with a touchup paintbrush may be too rough or noticeable. Depending on the color and type of paint finish, you may be better off carefully sanding scratches smooth and then feathering in new layers of fresh paint with an aerosol touchup can (available at some auto parts stores and auto body paint and supply outlets) or a regular spray-paint device.

PANEL PAINTING

With the possible exception of a few special automobiles, most vehicles are composed of a number of separate sections welded or bolted together. Professional auto body people generally refer to these sections as panels—for example, quarter panels and rear body panels.

In a lot of body collision or simple repaint situations, painters have to spray complete panels in lieu of spraying specific spots. Spot painting a number

Newer vehicles use paint and options tags to provide the paint code. On some vehicles, the VIN is included on this tag, while on others, it's located elsewhere. If you're having difficulty finding the paint and options tag, your auto paint and supply store should be able to offer assistance in determining where it's located on your vehicle.

of minor ding repairs scattered over an entire hood panel, for example, would probably turn out looking something like a leopard. This work would be much easier and the finished look much more uniform and professional if the entire hood were completely prepared and painted all at one time. Determining whether to spot paint or cover entire panels depends on the type and style of the existing paint finish, size of the repair area, and ability to blend new paint into the surrounding body paint area.

This Dodge sedan is almost masked sufficiently for the application of primer sufacer, which will extend beyond the repair area, yet not completely to the masked edge. The color coat will cover the entire left rear quarter panel, and both doors will be painted. To match the rest of the car, the painter may need to blend clear onto the trunk, roof, and front fender.

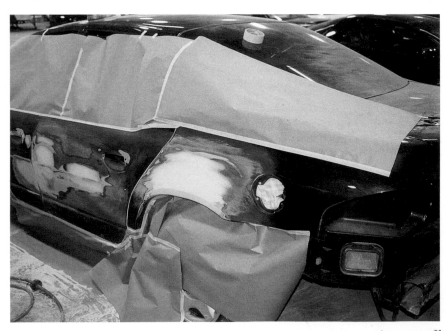

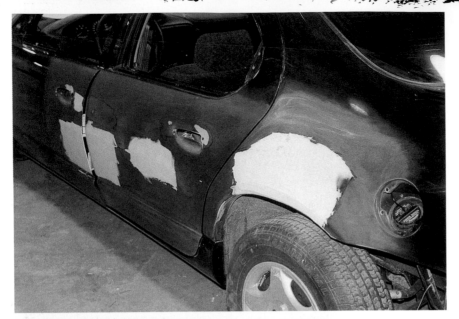

The areas of body filler show that this sedan had four small dents (two in each driver's side door) and a larger dent above the left rear wheel. If they were repainted separately, this car would look like a spotted leopard, so the entire side will be repainted.

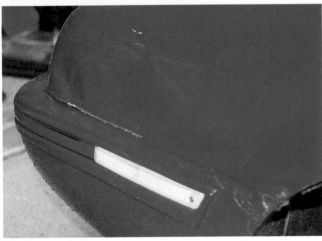

This is your typical fender bender that could be repaired by a novice bodyman. The fender is slightly wrinkled, but the sheet metal has no major creases. In days gone by, it would be necessary to remove the inner fender panel (and whatever accessories were in the way) and hammer the dent out from behind. Stud guns available now would allow you to weld small studs onto the outside of the fender, then use a slide hammer to pull the dent out. Either method would require at least a skim coat of body filler to finish the repair.

Some situations allow for painting just parts of panels, as opposed to entire units. These might include lower panel sections up to featured grooves, ridges, or trim lines on doors, fenders, or quarter panels. Special graphics or vinyl stripes might also serve as perimeters to cordon off particular areas, allowing for partial panel repaints. A ridge or trim line draws the eye away from the paint itself, making minor color variations unnoticeable.

With the advent of basecoat/clearcoat paint systems, color blending has all but eliminated panel painting. Even though the correct paint code may be known, the surface prepped properly, and the paint applied flawlessly, any panels painted separately from others will most likely not match the rest of the vehicle. Your ultimate goal is to apply paint in such a way that no definitive edges are visible, making that area appear as if it had never been repaired or repainted. Some single-panel repaint jobs require that adjacent panels on either side be lightly sprayed with feather coats of paint. This is done to help a primary painted panel's new finish blend in with surrounding panels.

Color blending can be done with single-stage paint products, but basecoat/clearcoat is recommended for the novice. Although the actual color of the repaired area may not match the adjacent panels exactly, the blend will create the illusion that the affected area was never damaged. On the other hand, two adjacent panels painted separately are quite noticeable when reinstalled on the vehicle.

COMPLETE PAINT JOB

On a partial repaint job, approximately 70 percent of the work involved is surface preparation, and only 30 percent is related to paint application. For a complete paint job, approximately 95 percent of the work is surface preparation, while only 5 percent is spent applying paint.

Many people do not understand that the condition of body surfaces prior to paint application directly affects the outcome of a paint job. Every speck of dirt, sanding scratch, pinhole, or other tiny

On this Dodge truck, a small portion of the passenger door required attention, and the roof had to be replaced because a tree fell across it. The small area of the door requiring bodywork was masked off from the rest of the door, although the entire door will receive paint before the repair is completed. When masking for actual paint application, the door or any other panel would never be masked with a square like this, unless the desired paint scheme called for a checkerboard pattern.

Before painting and even before most of the surface preparation, the bumpers, grille, door handles, mirrors, and everything else that could be removed were removed from this Ford pickup truck. The headlights will be left on in this case because masking paper will eventually cover the entire front of the vehicle.

blemish is magnified to a great extent after paint has been applied over it. The flawless, even quality of the surrounding paint draws the viewer's eye directly to the imperfection. Automotive paint, even in multiple layers, is still a very thin coating and simply will not cover up even minor flaws the way, say, house paint might. If it isn't smooth, don't spray it!

Complete paint jobs call for all exterior body trim to be removed. You should take off door handles, trim pieces, mirrors, emblems, badges, key locks, radio antennas, and anything else attached to your car's body. This reduces the need for intricate masking and prevents accidental overspray onto these pieces as a result of inadequate masking. Likewise, it allows paint to cover all vehicle body parts evenly and greatly reduces the chance of paint buildup or thin coat coverage on areas obstructed with handles, adornments, and add-ons.

Removing body trim and accessories requires hand tools to loosen nuts, bolts, and screws. Other pieces held in place by adhesives or double-backed tape may require an adhesive remover product. Take your time and remove items so that none of them are broken or damaged.

Once you start taking parts off your car, you'll probably be surprised at the number collected. In addition to door handles, key locks, and trim, you'll be removing light assemblies, reflectors, grille pieces, bumpers, license plates, mudguards, and a lot more. Therefore, develop a systematic storage plan, so nothing gets lost or broken.

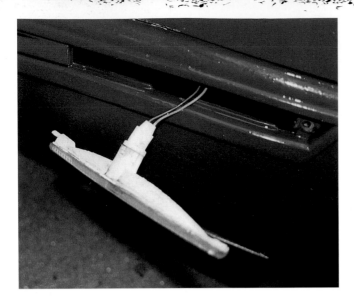

Most side marker lights are held into place by one or two small screws. Where Phillips screws were once common for this application, Torx head screws are typically found now. Make sure you use the proper type of screwdriver or tool. This particular light uses only one screw. The tab on one end is positioned into the opening, then the single screw holds the assembly in place. To completely remove the lens assembly, twist the bulb's socket while holding the lens assembly. The wires and the bulb can then be stuffed down into the opening in the fender to keep them out of the way.

Although much of the sheet metal in the engine compartment is blocked from plain view by the engine, accessories, and trim panels, it would be noticeable if it were a different color from the rest of the car. For that reason, think twice before attempting a color change paint job on a vehicle that isn't going to be completely disassembled. To paint the engine compartment correctly, you would remove the engine and accessories, steam clean the compartment, then perform the standard sheet-metal prep work. On a vintage restoration or hot rod project, that would be standard procedure, while on a daily driver, it most likely wouldn't be practical.

Have plenty of sturdy boxes on hand to store related parts as you take them off body areas. Keep fender parts together in one box, door items in another, and so forth. This way, when you start replacing them after paint work is completed, you'll be able to quickly and easily locate all necessary body and trim pieces as well as their fastening nuts, bolts, screws, clips, and so on. In addition to boxes, resealable freezer bags work well for temporary storage of small pieces and parts. Use a magic marker to note the contents on the storage label.

Expect to spend plenty of time sanding every square inch of your car or truck's body surface before picking up a spray gun. All imperfections must be smoothed or repaired to give paint a blemish-free bonding base. By itself, paint is not thick enough to hide sand scratch swelling or pinholes. For those problems, products such as primer sufacer are used, which also have to be sanded and smoothed to perfection if paint is expected to coat evenly and be visually attractive.

COLOR CHANGE PAINT JOB

Changing the color of a vehicle involves additional considerations. This is more difficult on some vehicles than others. For a complete color change, it will be necessary to paint the engine compartment, doorjambs, and interior. Unless you're extremely good with a detail gun and masking procedures, it will be necessary to remove the engine to repaint the engine compartment. If you're repainting a vehicle that already has the engine out, this is of little consequence, other than the additional sanding and surface preparation. This also holds true for the interior, although much of the interior will be covered by upholstery.

COLOR SELECTION

An important part of any paint job is picking the right color. If you're simply repairing and refinishing a dented fender on a late-model vehicle, this is not a big deal. However, if you're building that long-awaited hot rod or custom, the choice of a color may be more difficult than you would think. No matter what you're painting or how you go about choosing the color, look at your anticipated color under as many different lighting conditions as possible to make sure it's the right color for your vehicle.

Because so many different automotive paint colors are available to choose from, it may become confusing or downright frustrating trying to pick just

Whether your vehicle is a bone stocker or highly modified, with a minimal amount of searching you're bound to find at least one magazine that caters to your automotive interests. These magazines can be a great source of ideas for paint schemes and colors.

Contrary to popular belief, you don't always need flashy colors to stand out in a crowd. Longtime custom car painter Roger Ward painted his 1932 Ford roadster Nissan taupe (light tan) at a time when everyone else was painting their hot rods Porsche Red. His roadster stood out from the sea of red and still seems timeless when all those other cars have been repainted a time or two already.

one dynamic color for your car. Have patience. Look at issues of car and truck magazines to get ideas of the colors other enthusiasts are using. Attend car shows and talk to fellow car buffs about how they arrived at certain paint schemes. These conversations may lead you to good suppliers and products and also help you avoid mistakes your fellow enthusiasts already have made.

Many times, especially for older classic and vintage automobiles, certain color schemes prove more appealing than others. While a pink 1957 Thunderbird may be a head turner, an equally pink 1956 Oldsmobile may look out of place. Experienced car painters have a knack for envisioning the outcome of cars painted specific colors. From their experience around body shops and car shows and through reading thousands of auto magazines, they know which colors look best and are in style for most types of vehicles, from sports cars to pickups and late-model sedans to classic coupes.

If yours is an older project car that's finally ready for paint and you find yourself in a quandary as to what color to paint it, locate a local club whose members share an interest in the same make, model, or general vintage. A few casual conversations with them should help you to at least narrow your color choices to a select few. If there's any chance you may someday sell the vehicle, picking a color that's in keeping with its style and vintage may make it a hotter prospect.

MATCHING THE OLD

A word of caution about color codes printed on VIN or color and options tags is in order. Believe it or not, occasionally the codes do not match the color that was really sprayed on the vehicle. With the vast number of automobiles manufactured each year, the percentage that have incorrect codes is small but alarming. When you take the color code from your vehicle to the local automotive paint retailer to

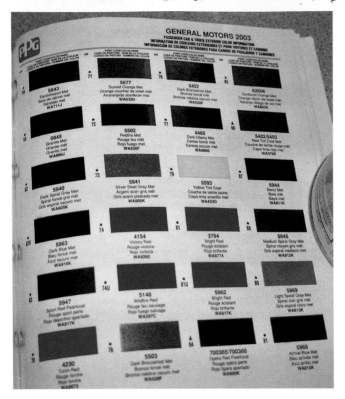

This photo of a 2003 General Motors color chart shows five similar shades of red, and other colors also have similar shades. The "plain" red for a Chevrolet may be different from the red on a Buick or a Pontiac. Although they may look the same in a paint chip book, they can be noticeably different when sprayed side by side. Some colors shown in the sample book are for underhood or interior use and will not have as much gloss. Before you select a color, view it in sunlight, not just the store's fluorescent lighting.

purchase paint, tell them the basic color of the vehicle. If the color code you supply yields yellow paint but your car is black, the paint jobber will want to know before mixing a gallon or two of paint that you won't be able to use.

If this happens, you can choose a color from a large selection of paint selection charts. Automotive paint shops have volumes of OEM paint chips categorized by year and vehicle manufacturer. If you're looking for paint to match a 2003 Chevrolet Monte Carlo for example, you could go to the 2003 General Motors portion of the paint selection chart and probably find what you're looking for.

Similar colors from different years or manufacturers may be close yet somewhat different. When you find a color that looks close, ask the painter if the color you selected is actually for a Monte Carlo. The color you selected may be for a Camaro or a Corvette but not the correct color for your Monte

Carlo. When there were fewer colors for cars, finding an exact match was much easier.

Another reality is that for each color code, multiple formulas will provide paint acceptable by the vehicle manufacturer. The reason is the robotic paint process used by vehicle manufacturers. As an example, the first 10 vehicles going down the paint line are supposed to be black, followed by 10 that are supposed to be white, 10 red, 10 yellow, and 10 blue.

By computer control, the paint spraying system is purged at each color change. In our example, 9 of the first 10 vehicles will be black, but the tenth will be slightly lighter than the 9 before it. The first two or three white vehicles will be slightly grayer than the middleones, while those at the end of the white session will be slightly pink, due to the red in the system.

Of the red vehicles, the first few won't be as vibrant as the heart of the run, while the end of the run will have more of a yellow cast or orange appearance to them. Of course, the yellow vehicles are affected also. The first few may yield a "dirty" yellow compared to the middle of the batch or the slightly green-appearing vehicles that would result from the end of the yellow run.

This characteristic is not limited to any one manufacturer or color, although certain colors of certain vehicles are more commonplace. For any color code entered in the paint formula database, a prime formula is displayed. Formulas for all known variants of this same color code are also displayed. Each variant has a code that indicates such properties as "less red, more yellow" or "less white, more red." Some color codes may not have variant codes, while some may have ten.

When a color code has variant color codes listed, the person mixing the paint will always supply the paint from the prime formula if the paint is intended for a complete paint job. If the paint is for a repair, color chips from each of the variant colors must be compared to the vehicle to be repaired to obtain the correct color.

A second method of determining the paint formula for virtually any color found on an automobile involves the use of a color spectrometer. This is an expensive tool that the average paint retailer will not have but may be able to gain access to through their paint distributor. If you're trying to match a color that can't be found through available paint codes, the extra effort of finding a color spectrometer may be the answer.

A portion of the vehicle with the desired paint color is scanned, using the color spectrometer. The information gathered by the spectrometer is then downloaded into a computer, which deciphers the color and displays the appropriate paint formula. Although paint matching cannot be 100 percent accurate all the time, this process is extremely accurate on single-stage or two-stage paints. However, it is not designed for nor capable of determining the formula of tri-stage paints or finishes that include special-effect additives, such as pearl or metallic.

Auto body paint and supply stores can match almost any color of automotive paint. However, if you want a specific color not displayed in any color chart or paint chip catalog, it will have to be made by hand using trial and error. Expect to pay a lot more for this service than for stock colors because of the added labor involved.

This situation arises when you request a color match with a repainted car and have no idea what color was used or who did the work. In those cases, jobbers will simply ask you to search through volumes of color chips until you find the closest match. Then they work with specific tints until they produce a suitable color. Unless you find a paint chip that perfectly matches that car, they mix paint by hand until they find a match, which may require hours. This is why special, hand-matched colors cost a lot more than standard quantities of those colors whose formulas are stored in company computers.

SELECTING THE NEW

Selecting a new color for the complete repaint of a vehicle might not be quite as easy. Valspar Refinish already has 100,000 different automotive paint colors on file, and its engineers are kept busy using computer science and experience in graphic arts to develop new hues. The days of walking into a paint store and simply asking for a quart of red paint are gone. Today, there are easily over 600 different shades of red, so customers must be a lot more specific. They need to pick out a certain color chip from any number of color catalogs or have a particular paint code number available. Most other colors have as many variations.

One way to decide on a new paint color is to visit local automobile dealerships. When you find a car or truck with a paint scheme you like, copy the vehicle's numerical paint code and take it to your local auto body paint and supply store. In lieu of paint codes,

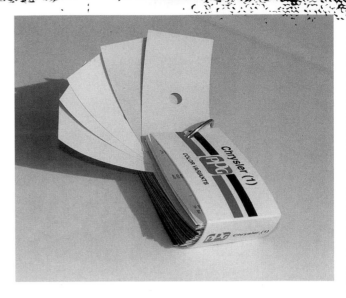

Although difficult to distinguish in the photo, all five variant chips are slightly different but are all for the same paint code. You place the card on your car and compare its color to the surrounding shade through the hole in the middle. After determining that the vehicle you're painting is the prime color or a variant thereof, make note of it for future reference, in case you need to purchase additional paint for that vehicle at some other time.

proper paint mixing formulas may be located on computer files with just the year, make, and model of most newer vehicles. Customers can confirm colors by comparing that information with corresponding color chips from paint color catalogs.

CUSTOM FINISHES

Along with color selection, you may want to investigate special custom paint additives. Metallics have improved since their heyday in the 1960s. Now, instead of large, bold flakes loudly accenting a car body, you can add specific doses of tiny microflakes to make an otherwise bland color light up to a magnificent and brilliant finish. A good number of newer car paint finishes include tiny metallics. You can see them firsthand on automobiles at almost any new car dealership or on color chips at your local auto body paint and supply store.

Pearl additives are another means by which you can make a solid color look custom. In years past, fish scales were used to give stock colors a pearlescent appearance that made them look different shades when viewed from various angles. In essence, a vehicle that might appear white when viewed straight on may offer a bright pink or blue shade when seen from a lower angle or from the front or back.

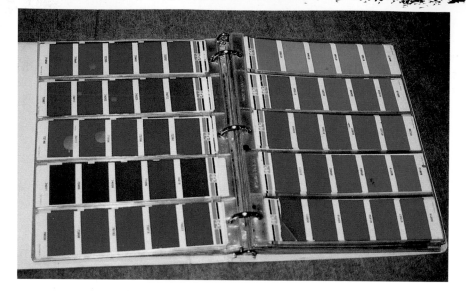

If you're not looking to match an OEM color or for a metallic or pearl, you may decide to go with a fleet color for your repainting project. This is a sample book of virtually every color of vehicle paint imaginable, although they're all solid colors—no pearls, metallics, or other "custom" additives. This is just one page of predominantly red paints, with a few more pages of reds in the book and several other pages of predominantly yellows, blues, and shades of gray.

Body filler and primer sufacers must be allowed to dry fully before you apply additional fillers or topcoats. Painters often use heat lamps to speed up the process. This truck has had some sheet metal straightened, some body filler added, and some primer sufacer applied. The current coat of primer sufacer is being dried with a heat lamp.

Today's pearl additives are made by applying oxide pigments to micaceous iron oxide (mica) or aluminum. These tiny chips may be painted on one side while remaining clear on the other. Depending on the pearl color selected and the angle of light reflection from your viewpoint, these paint jobs can offer unique perspectives.

It used to be that for spot repairs, manufacturers of these products would advise repainting the entire affected side of the vehicle, from headlight to taillight. This is so each part of the full side will display identical tints from all directions and not cause clouds of varying degrees between panels or parts of panels. With improvements in pearl products and stricter standards, these paints are now easier to blend for spot repairs than just a few years ago. Today, the only real drawback to a pearl finish is that it absolutely must be clearcoated for long-term color stability.

Special paint systems using metallics and pearls can be satisfactorily applied by novice painters who follow all label instructions and tips from application guides. Take advantage of this wealth of information at your fingertips to make your paint job progress as expected.

CONSULTANTS

Besides choosing what color to paint your car or truck, possibly the biggest decision is whether to paint it yourself or pay someone else to do the work. Before you simply jump in (and possibly get in way over your head before you know it), first find out what your choices are and what they will cost. If you want to get your daily driver painted but don't have the proper equipment or the necessary time, you may be better off to have the work done by a reputable shop.

TALKING WITH A PROFESSIONAL AUTO PAINTER

Automobile owners with little or no knowledge of the auto body repair and paint business are frequently surprised at the cost of a quality paint job. They have no idea of the amount of work involved during preparation stages before painting, nor of the cost of materials such as primers, sealers, reducers, hardeners, and paint. Uninformed car owners have a difficult time understanding why some companies can paint cars for as little as $99.95 while other shops might charge around $5,000 or more for a top-notch, complete paint job. Of course, the price of a paint job has no real ceiling because the labor involved will vary greatly, depending on what you need done.

If you decide to have a professional paint your car, remember that you get what you pay for. Outfits that specialize in cheap paint jobs cannot afford to spend a lot of time preparing or masking cars. Their business relies on volume. The more cars they paint, the more money they make. Therefore, sanding and masking work is normally minimal.

Close inspection of vehicles that have been repainted by inexpensive paint shops generally reveals overspray on fenderwells, leaf springs, emblems, badges, window trim, spare tires under pickup truck beds, and the like, due to minimal masking. Rough surface spots may receive a quick pass or two with sandpaper, but extra time cannot be allotted for definitive sanding and feathering. These shops are not going to remove the bed from your pickup truck to paint the back of the cab, either.

If you want a much more thorough paint job than the one just described, and most people do, these shops can provide better-quality service. This will, of course, cost you more, with the price of "extras" quickly approaching that of a more thorough, lower-volume shop. Inexpensive paint shops are forced to use bulk supplies. Color choices are usually limited to the colors on hand in 55-gallon barrels. Frequently, shops like these will buy out paint manufacturers' supplies of discontinued colors at huge discounts. They pass this savings on to you. In many cases, enamel-based products are used because they cover in one or two coats and don't require rubbing out or polishing afterward.

Auto paint shops that specialize in overall quality and customer satisfaction are vastly different from high-volume shops. You'll have to pay more for their service, but your car or truck will be meticulously prepared and then painted with a high-quality, durable paint. All exterior accessories will be removed, including bumpers and grille. Masking will be complete, and work required after spraying will be accomplished professionally.

Once the surface has been meticulously smoothed, coats of sealer are sprayed on, to protect undercoats from absorbing potent solvents included in paint. Sufficient drying time must be allotted. Professionals often use high-intensity heat lamps to speed this process. These lamps use a tremendous amount of electricity, which must be figured into estimates as part of the overhead costs.

After that phase has been completed, color coats are applied and then cured with assistance from heat lamps. Depending on the type of paint system used, clearcoats might be sprayed over the entire vehicle. Normally, three coats are enough. When the clear has dried, painters carefully inspect car bodies for imperfections. Then 1200 to 2000-grit sandpaper is used to smooth blemishes, as needed, and additional coats of clear may be applied.

Satisfied that their job has turned out correctly, painters buff entire vehicle bodies with fine polish and a soft buffing pad. After all of that has been done, parts still have to be replaced. Again, this takes time, as gaskets and seals must be perfectly positioned to function as intended. Care must be taken so that parts are not bumped against newly painted finishes to cause nicks or scratches.

As if that weren't enough, each vehicle is then detailed to perfection. I doubt many customers would pay their paint bill if glass, wheels, tires, weatherstripping, and other parts were dirty and covered with sanding dust when they arrived to pick up the car. Most quality body shop owners insist that their customers' cars be detailed before delivery. Their customers enjoy a freshly painted car and can relish the fact that it has been cleaned to perfection. The car stands out, looks crisp, and is a pleasure to drive.

When shopping for a professional auto painter, be sure to ask if your car will be detailed before delivery. Ask if all exterior accessories will be removed for painting and whether overspray to fenderwells and suspension assemblies will be removed or painted over. Be certain that maximum attention will be given to masking and that quality paint products will be used throughout the job.

Finding a professional auto paint shop with a reputable track record should not be too difficult. Word-of-mouth recommendations are generally

This small portion of the stock room at the paint store contains just about everything you could possibly need for painting your vehicle-sandpaper, masking tape, paint spray guns, respirators, paint, and primer.

Virtually any color you could imagine can be mixed from the toners on these shelves. After choosing a color, you could decide to have it in a base/clear system, a single-stage urethane, an acrylic lacquer, or an acrylic enamel. Few colors are actually stocked in a ready-to-use mix, as shelf space would quickly be depleted.

reliable. If a friend or neighbor has recently had a car painted, ask how he or she feels about the quality of service. You can also talk to your auto insurance agent, fellow car enthusiasts, a local detailer, or your mechanic.

You might even ask the owner of a local specialty auto sales business. These folks are true auto enthusiasts—they have to be, to stay up to date on the latest classic car trends and make the best deals when it comes to the sale of classic and vintage automobiles. To them, a less than professional auto bodyshop is a nightmare. They expect to pay higher prices for quality work, but in return, they demand that work be of the highest caliber. Dealers in this business get a lot of money for the cars they sell.

Your telephone book's yellow pages are loaded with auto body repair and paint shop advertisements. Call a few of the shops to get a feel for their professionalism over the phone. As you cut your list to three or four, take time to visit selected facilities, to see firsthand what kind of operation they conduct. You should expect courteous and knowledgeable estimators and organized, well-lighted, tidy work areas. Talk to estimators and ask direct questions. Get estimates from each shop before committing to one. At the end of the day, compare prices and select the shop that offered the best service for the most equitable price.

AUTO BODY PAINT AND SUPPLY STORE

Auto body paint and supply stores are in business to keep body shops adequately supplied in paint products, body repair materials, and tools for both types of work. The jobbers who work in these stores are constantly updated with product information from manufacturers of paint and body repair supplies. Although some jobbers may never have actually painted cars, their technical knowledge of paint product use is second to none.

Novice auto painters can learn a great deal from jobbers when both parties fully comprehend the paint project at hand. Be up front and honest with the jobber. If possible, bring your car to the store's location so the jobber can see your project firsthand. This way, he can best recommend a proper paint system to use and supplies you'll need to complete the job.

Don't expect jobbers to drop everything just to give you lessons in painting cars. Their primary job is to serve professional body shops, not teach auto painting. For the most part, Mondays and Fridays are their busiest days. Shop owners generally call in orders on Monday for supplies they'll need for the week's work. On Friday, shops may need special deliveries of materials to complete jobs that customers expect to pick up that afternoon. So plan to visit an auto body supply store during midweek, when jobbers may have more time to converse with you.

In addition to stocking everything from paint guns to sandpaper, auto body paint and supply stores carry information sheets and application guides on almost all of the paint-related products they sell. Paint manufacturers provide this material. You can get sheets on the use and application of primer sufacers, sealers, and tri-stage paint systems, as well as just about every other product you might ever put on your car's body. They're free, so take one for every product you intend to use.

Unless you have experience painting cars, you might ask your auto body paint and supply jobber how much sandpaper of which grit you'll need to properly prepare your car's finish for new paint. Sanding chores are different with each job, and fine-grit paper doesn't last as long as you might expect. Along with sandpaper, buy plenty of automotive paint masking tape and paper. Two-inch tape works great for some chores, while 3/4-inch and 1/8-inch works better for more detailed tasks.

By and large, your auto body paint and supply store jobber can be a fountain of information. Take advantage of this person's knowledge by being polite and courteous and by asking intelligent questions. Be aware of the store's busiest hours and plan to visit during slack times.

SPECIAL CONSIDERATIONS

Automotive painting has become a high-tech business. Not only do painters have to be concerned about the finished product, they must also be keenly aware of personal safety hazards involved with potent chemicals used in paint bases and hardeners. Where filter masks proved to be health-conscious aids a few years ago, positive-pressure respirators are state of the art now. Be aware of fire hazards, especially pilot lights on hot water heaters and home heating systems. Thinners and reducers are highly flammable, so be sure cigarettes and other sources of ignition are kept far away from your project.

laying down the
BASE COAT

BY DENNIS PARKS

How you apply the paint is every bit as important as the quality of the paint itself. Before you start spraying on your carefully prepped vehicle, get a used door, hood, or trunk lid and practice the art of laying on paint smoothly and evenly. You're not just developing your own skills; you're also learning how your equipment performs its job. Leave the runs, drips, and irregularities on your practice panel and shoot your vehicle like a pro.

Another thing to consider before mixing the paint and filling your gun is to highlight certain time recommendations and other important data that came with your paint system, so you can refer to them during your job. If you prepare a small outline, including all the painting and drying steps in sequential order, you can check off each step once you've completed it. If you like to multitask or have kids, a cell phone, or other distractions, this approach will help you remember what you've done, what you need to do, and how much time you have to do it. Try using something other than a typical sheet of paper for this, such as an off-size piece of light cardboard or a colored sheet, and you'll be able to distinguish it quickly among any other notes or papers.

Mix your paint products according to label instructions and apply them at the recommended air pressure. Try painting with different fan patterns and pressure settings to see which combinations work best for intricate work in confined spaces and which perform better on large panels. Practice holding paint guns at perpendicular angles to work surfaces; see what happens when you don't. Use cans of inexpensive paint, and practice until you become familiar with the techniques required for good paint coverage. When the paint has dried, practice wet sanding, rubbing out, and buffing.

Practice with your new dual-action sander to remove those coats of paint. Put a deep scratch in your practice panel and repair it, instead of practicing on your favorite car or truck. Become proficient with the tools and materials you expect to use while fixing your special car before attacking its precious surface with power tools and harsh chemicals. Practice, practice, and practice some more. Once it looks good on your practice panel, you know you're ready for the big time.

PAINT MIXING

Because there are tens of thousands of different automotive paint colors, mixing the correct shade for your car is a precise science. Following stock vehicle color codes or those selected from paint chip catalogs, auto body paint and supply personnel measure drops of color tint to the tenth of a gram to create the prescribed colors. They do this work for you as part of your paint system purchase.

Paint materials are shipped in concentrated form, which helps keep the heavy pigments and other solid materials from settling. Painters then add solvents to make those products sprayable. Remember that the atmospheric conditions at which you spray the paint also affect the thinners or reducers you need to add. By shipping the paint in concentrated form and allowing end users to mix and dilute it as necessary, according to suppliers' instructions, manufacturers help ensure that painters in any region and climate can get precisely the paint and mixture they need for best results.

In most cases, you'll have to dilute concentrated paint with solvent (thinner or reducer) to yield a sprayable mixture. You must also add specific quantities of hardener to those products that call for it. Be careful—once you mix in hardener, the hardening process begins. Catalyzed paint has a limited shelf life, which your paint system's instructions will explain.

Take the following steps to be sure you get the right paint mixture. First, read the instructions that came with the paint system. Next, read the

Before spraying paint, you need a suitable area for mixing, reducing, and then pouring the paint into your spray gun. This spacious, stainless-steel-topped table provides plenty of room and is relatively easy to keep clean. A wooden workbench will provide the same results for the hobbyist, but this is a glimpse of the ideal setup. At the middle of the photo are two stands for holding gravity-feed spray guns while paint is poured into the paint cup. At the back of the table are the various reducers and cans used for mixing. At the far end is a selection of pearl additives.

Also located in the mixing room is a 55-gallon drum that serves as a receptacle for excess paint, reducers, and other solvents. Any time a spray gun is cleaned, additional solvents are added to this. The body shop then has to have these products disposed of on a regular basis. For the hobbyist, disposal may present more of a problem, depending on where you live. Many paint distributors will accept small amounts of solvents from their customers, sometimes for a small fee. If it's not convenient to return the waste solvents to where you bought them, check with your local authorities to determine proper disposal methods.

instructions that came with your spray gun and air compressor. These two sources should give you a strong sense of the mixture ratio you'll need. Then, before you mix, run any questions you may have past the paint supplier from whom you got your paint. By checking and crosschecking in this manner, you'll be sure you have just the right mixture for your application, climate, and equipment.

For the mixing process itself, paint manufacturers have designed calibrated mixing sticks. According to the mixing directions, pour an amount of paint into a clean, empty can with straight sides (not a spray-gun cup), up to a certain number located along one vertical column on that paint system's designated mixing stick. Then pour solvent in until the fluid level in the can rises to a corresponding number on the next

column over on the same stick. Clear mixing cups with calibrations printed on them are used in the same manner as mixing sticks.

If you need a one-to-one ratio of paint to solvent, for example, pour paint into an empty can up to the number one. Then add reducer until the mixture reaches the number one on the next column over. If you need more paint for a large job, simply mix the ingredients up to a higher number—again, following the ratios your particular system and circumstances indicate.

If your paint system requires mixing paint, solvent, and hardener, it will use a mixing stick with three columns instead of two—one for each ingredient. Pour paint up to the desired number on the paint column, solvent to the appropriate number in that column, and hardener to its corresponding number.

Not all paint systems are based on a one-to-one ratio. By looking at a paint-mixing stick, you'll see that sometimes the numbers on the reducer or hardener are not twice as high up the stick as those in the paint column. Measuring sticks provide an accurate way of mixing paint, solvent, and hardener. Follow the manufacturer's recommendations and instructions to be assured of a quality blend.

Once you've blended your paint product, use the stir stick to swish the contents around in the mixing can. Pointed tools, such as screwdrivers, don't work well for stirring. You want something flat-bottomed and rather wide—hence the stir stick. Stir for at least 2 minutes. Then place a paint filter over the opening of your spray-gun cup and pour in the mixture.

Never, repeat, *never*, pour paint into your spray-gun cup without using some type of filter. An impurity passed into your gun could cause it to misspray or clog, creating a lot of extra work fixing the paint surface and your spray gun.

Your paint product is now ready for spraying. Be sure to put the caps back on containers of solvent, hardener, and paint. This will prevent unnecessary evaporation or accidental spillage.

In the paint booth, tack off your car or truck's surface immediately. Then start painting. Some paint products and colors are designed with a lot of heavy solids that could settle to the bottom of paint cups in just 10 to 15 minutes. If you were to take your time tacking and get distracted while your paint gun sat idle, solids could settle, possibly causing the color to change. This would be a catastrophe, especially with spot paint repairs.

Custom paint mixing (when a formula is available) has always been done by weight. The paint formula provides a starting amount of base color, which is poured into the appropriate-sized paint can. The second toner is added until the weight matches the given total for the two parts. Third and successive toners are added in the same manner, until the sum of the parts equals the total amount. An electronic digital scale is much easier for this process than an old-fashioned beam scale.

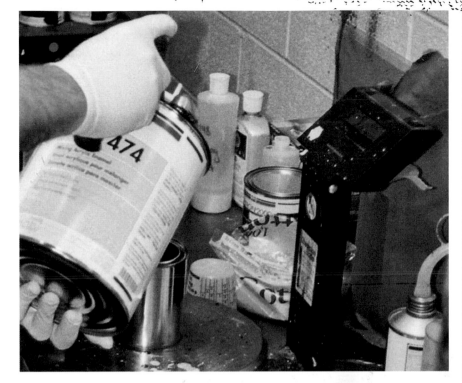

Once the various toners specified in a paint formula are combined, they must be mixed sufficiently by vigorous agitation in a paint shaker. It will also be necessary for you to stir the paint prior to use because the solvents will settle to the bottom as it sits on the shelf.

SPRAY-GUN CONTROLS AND TEST PATTERNS

Paint companies recommend specific spray-gun setups for applying their products. A sample recommendation for the DeVilbiss JGV-572 base coat spray gun is "Fluid Tip—FW (0.062 in.); Air Cap #86." This would indicate a specific fluid tip and air cap that should be used with this particular paint product and would be available from the dealer of the spray gun. This is another reason to purchase your spray gun from a paint supply outlet, rather than a tool store that sells a variety of tools without servicing any of them. A similar recommendation would apply to primer and clearcoat spray guns by the same manufacturer, Sata or Sharpe. These settings are available from information sheets and application guidelines or from your auto body paint and supply jobber.

Most full-size production spray-paint guns have two control knobs. One controls the fan spray, while the other manages the volume of paint that exits the nozzle. They're located at the top rear section of most models. About the only way to achieve proper spray patterns and volume is to practice spraying paint on a test panel. Various paint products and their reduction ratios will spray differently, especially with different recommended air pressures.

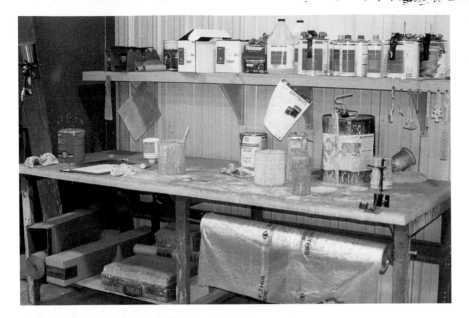

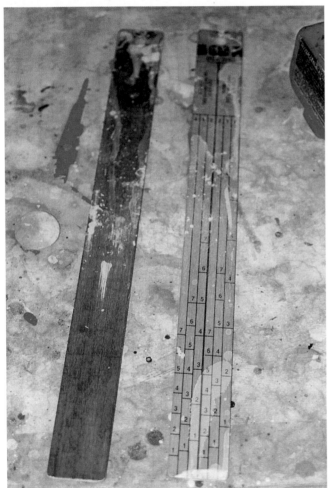

Technological advances make today's paint products very user-friendly. If you prepare the surface correctly, mix the products correctly, and apply them correctly, they will yield a good paint job. Proper mixing ratios are included with the product information sheets, and calibrated mixing cups or measuring sticks are available from your paint store.

Many painters keep test panels in their spray-paint booth. Usually, these are nothing more than sheets of wide masking paper taped to a wall. They can spray paint on the test panel and then adjust the gun's control knobs to get the right pattern and volume. At that point, they begin painting.

Periodically during paint jobs, painters may notice a flaw in their gun's fan pattern. To check it, they turn to the test panel and shoot a clean section with a mist of paint. If it looks off, they check the controls and air pressure. If the pattern is still flawed, they disconnect the paint gun from the supply hose and clean it. Chances are, a small port or passage has become clogged and must be cleaned before they can continue the job.

As the surface to be painted becomes more confined or difficult, such as on some front-end sections, painters must reduce pressure or change fan sprays to hit a smaller area. They make these adjustments with the help of the test panel.

SPRAY-GUN MANEUVERING

You've secured two essential components for your project: good paint and a quality spray gun. But those essentials alone won't get you a great paint job. How you apply the paint is just as important. Spray-paint guns typically work best when held perpendicular to the surface being sprayed, at a distance of 6–10 inches; check the recommendations for your gun.

PPG's *Refinish Manual* has this caution for painters: "If the gun is tilted toward the surface, the fan pattern won't be uniform. If the gun is swung in an arc, varying the distance from the nozzle to the work, the paint will go on wetter (and thicker) where the nozzle is

Most body shops have special dispenser caps that allow them to pour the desired amount of paint into the mixing cup. These are a convenience, but not necessary. However, you will undoubtedly find that pouring from a quart can is much easier than from a full gallon can. Enough sealer (in this case) for the next application is poured into the mixing cup to a predetermined line on the mixing cup. Reducer is added until the total mixture comes to the same numbered line in the next column marking the appropriate ratio.

closer to the surface and drier (and thinner) where it is farther away." If the outer layers of the thick, wetter paint dry before the inner layers, the solvent evaporating from within will cause defects in the finish. At the far end of the arc, the paint will go on too thin to provide adequate coverage or may be too dry by the time it hits the surface, resulting in something more like overspray than a proper coat of paint.

About the only time painters do fan the paint gun is on small spot repaints. These spots call for full coverage in the center and less paint around their feathered perimeter, where it blends with existing paint. This is done with wrist action to lightly blend edges only. Practice this technique on a test panel before attempting it on your car or truck.

Because automobile roofs, hoods, and trunk lids lie in a horizontal plane, hold the paint gun at a horizontal angle and make smooth, even, uniform passes. To prevent paint from dripping on the body, many painters tie an old tack cloth or other absorbent and lint-free rag around the top of the cup, where it makes contact with its support base. Even with paint guns that are reported to be dripless, this is not a bad idea.

Holding the paint gun so the nozzle is perpendicular to the surface is important. Lock your wrist and elbow, then walk along panels to ensure a right-angle position. Do not rely solely upon your arm to swing back and forth. Move your body with your arm and shoulder anchored. Again, this takes practice, especially when you have to move from one panel to another in a smooth, steady, even walk.

The mixture is then stirred for a couple of minutes, using a paint stir stick. Don't attempt to use a screwdriver for this. The blade isn't wide enough to stir anything, and it ruins the screwdriver. Stirring sticks are available where you purchase your paint, so make sure you ask for a few when you pick up supplies.

Even fan spray should overlap the previous spray by half. In other words, the center of the first pass should be directed along the masking line: half of the paint on the masking paper, the other half on the body surface. The second pass should be directed in such a way that the top of the fan rides right along the masking line. Then, each successive pass should overlap the previous one by half. Maneuver each pass

With the gravity-feed gun securely supported in the stand and a paint strainer in place atop the paint cup, the sealer can be poured into the paint cup. For most suction-feed guns, the stand isn't necessary because the bottom of the paint cup is large enough to stand on its own. No matter what you're spraying, make sure you use a paint strainer when pouring it into your paint cup. Also, make sure you put the cap back on the spray-paint gun and secure it properly. With the air pressure involved when spraying paint, an unsecured paint cap can make a mess.

with the same speed and at the same distance away from the surface: 6–10 inches.

Look at your painting results. If you have practiced with your equipment on an old hood or trunk lid, chances are good that your efforts are proving worthwhile. If not, you might be experiencing runs or other gross abnormalities. Runs are generally caused by too much paint landing on the surface at one time. You may be holding the gun too close or walking too slowly. Whichever, you have to adjust. Keep practicing until the paint appears to go on smoothly and evenly without running.

SPOT PAINTING

Whether your project involves a minor body repair or complete repaint, the rules of right-angle application and controlled spraying remain in effect. The difference is in the amount of paint needed and the technique for blending new paint into old finishes.

What you want to avoid when spot painting is a raised line separating the section you painted from the old surface. One way to get around this problem is to mask along a definite edge, groove, vinyl graphic, or stripe. Depending on the type of paint you use and the prominence of the lip or raised paint edge, some delicate wet sanding could make the scar almost invisible. Professionals opt for a different method. First, they mask an edge or stopping point with tape rolled over on itself.

Let's say you want to spot paint a ding repair near the driver's side taillight on the quarter panel. You've masked along a piece of bodyside molding on the

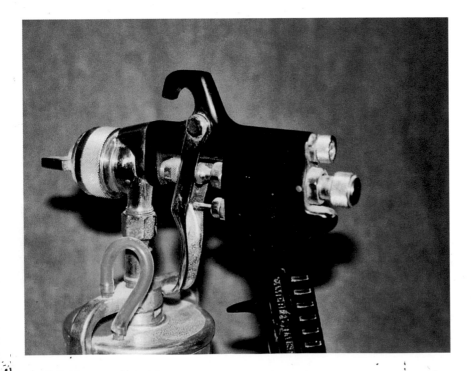

The two knobs on the back of the spray-gun housing are for adjusting the paint material and the airflow. Material control is usually adjusted by the knob in line with the air nozzle, while the airflow is adjusted by the opposite knob. Refer to the literature included with your spray gun or ask your salesman if you have any questions regarding adjusting or cleaning your spray gun. This is all the more reason to purchase a spray gun from an auto body paint and supply store rather than a discount store. When adjusted properly, most spray guns will give great results and, if cleaned and maintained correctly, will last indefinitely.

This parts-holding rack is designed to tilt and adjust as necessary for the parts being painted. These are common in body shops but are probably too expensive for the hobbyist painting his first car. Although not actually the case in this photo, it appears as though the upper portion of the rack would interfere with the spray gun while the painter sprays this bumper. This is something you must consider when laying out or hanging parts to be painted. They must be situated so that you can access them completely. Anything that cannot be adequately covered will require repositioning after the part has dried, to allow you to paint the opposite side or anything that was not accessible.

Attempt to position parts to be painted so that as much of the part as possible can be painted from a comfortable position. This won't always be possible, but make it easy on yourself when you can.

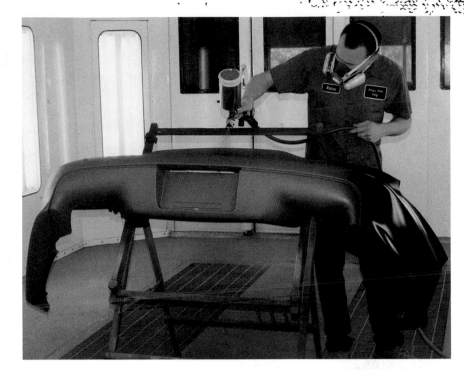

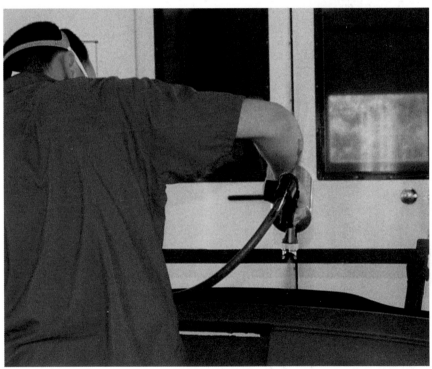

bottom of the panel and a design groove on the top. But toward the front and back, there are no definite break points. To solve this problem, lay a piece of masking paper at both the front and rear ends of the repair area, as if they were going to cover more of the paint surface than needed. Affix the front tape edge of the piece toward the front and the rear tape edge of the piece toward the rear.

Now, roll the paper over the tape edge so that only the sticky side of the tape is exposed. In other words roll the front section of paper toward the front

of the car, over the secured tape edge, and roll the rear section of paper toward the rear of the car. This leaves the repair area clear and both the front and rear areas masked with a strip of tape that has been rolled back over itself.

The purpose of this technique is to create a curved section of tape that paint can bounce off of and become overspray, with only a portion of it actually adhering to the surface. This prevents the paint from forming a well-defined line along the tape and helps it feather into a great blend.

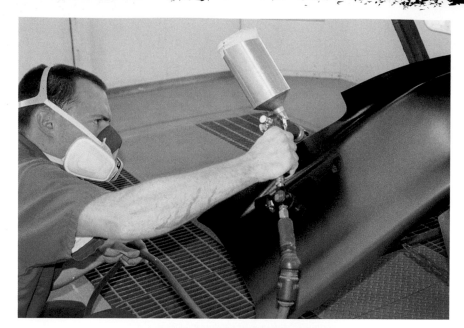

To avoid having excess paint that causes runs, and dry spots that don't cover, it's essential to hold the spray gun perpendicular to the surface being painted, even if you have to kneel down or stand on a stepladder. This will put you in a better position to see what you're doing. Notice also how the free hand is holding the air hose well away from the parts being painted.

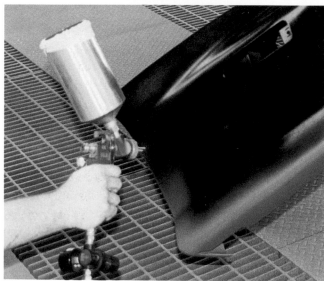

Unless you're painting a very small part, you'll need to move around to see and paint all surfaces. When you think you have all surfaces covered, it's a good idea to walk around the pieces or parts again, looking from different angles to make sure you have indeed covered all you intended.

To help that kind of situation even more, painters like to reduce paint to about a three-to-one ratio for melting. Once they've painted the spot, they remove those rolled-over strips of paper and tape and then empty their paint gun cups to about 1/4 inch full. To that, they add 3/4 inch of reducer. This makes for a very hot mixture, a blend that will loosen old paint and allow just a tint of the new paint to melt in. The results are great because it's difficult to find where the new paint starts and the old paint leaves off. If any nibs remain, you can wet sand them smooth, unless you've used uncatalyzed enamel paint.

The most important thing to remember about spot painting is that a valley has to be filled where you removed the old paint and sealer. It might only be 1–3 mils deep, but nevertheless, it has to be filled if the overall surface is to be flat, even, and smooth. New sealer and primer sufacer will fill up most of the valley, with paint filling in the rest and then blending with the adjacent surface.

The reducer-rich paint mixture literally opens up the existing paint to let a touch of new pigment fall into place and blend with the old. This is the last step of a paint job, after the appropriate flash (drying) time has passed for the final spray-paint pass for the center of the repaint.

Warning! Before attempting this kind of spot repair technique on your car, confirm its value with your auto body paint and supply specialist. It works great for some urethanes and lacquers, but it may not fare so well with certain enamels. It all depends on the brand and type of product you use, the paint currently on your car, the color, and what additives, such as metallic or pearl, are involved. There is no clear-cut rule to follow—each case is unique.

FULL-PANEL PAINTING

Automobile and paint manufacturers advise auto painters to repaint complete sides of certain cars, even if the only problem area is minor body repair on a single panel. As ridiculous as this sounds, there is a method to the madness. This type of overkill repaint involves vehicles factory painted with pearl or other special additives. Tricoat or candy finishes are also extremely difficult to match with new paint because of

When spraying a large, flat area, the panel you're painting should be either horizontal or vertical rather than at an angle. When spraying the side of a vehicle, it will basically be vertical, while the top, trunk, and deck lid will be horizontal. Depending on your stature, you may have difficulty reaching the middle of some large panels, such as the hood or deck lid from some of the land barges of the 1950s and 1960s. In that event, you may want to remove the panel, to be sure you get an even coat.

the complex interplay of coatings that produces the finish's unique look.

To find out whether your finish is amenable to spot painting—new-style paint schemes are more likely to be difficult—check with your local auto body paint and supply store.

Painting just a panel or two is generally no big deal with noncustom paint products. Masking can begin and end on definite body design breaks. You can see what has to be painted and know that virtually everything else has to be masked. But what if your car or truck is a little on the old side and you're concerned about matching the new color with the old? Who wants a door and fender to look like new while the quarter panel, hood, and roof look old and oxidized?

Many times, a complete buff job on old paint surfaces makes them look just like the new paint that was just sprayed onto doors and fenders. In other cases, you must spray a blend to feather in between the new paint and the old.

Feathering in is similar to the melting-in process described earlier—melting-in describes this process on a single panel, whereas feathering is blending surrounding panels to match the one that was repaired or refinished. After a panel is completely painted, you remove the masking and spray a light coating of heavily reduced paint and reducer onto the existing paint. This works well for certain products but not at all for others. Check with your auto body paint supplier to see if your new paint can be feathered into the existing paint in this manner.

To blend in panels with compatible paint finishes, painters complete their main job and then take off strips of masking from adjoining panels. With a heavily

reduced paint mix, they gently melt in a feathered edge. These edges may extend out to 6 inches. When the paint finishes are incompatible for melting, painters must rely on a perfect color match between adjacent panels.

FLASH TIMES

Paint dries as its solvents evaporate and its pigments cure. You cannot spray additional coats until the solvents from the first coat, and each successive coat, have had adequate time to evaporate. This is critical! If you spray a new coat of paint over one that has not had time to flash (dry), you will be trapping solvents underneath the new layer. They will not remain harmlessly in place but will pass through the overlying material, causing blistering, checking, crazing, cracking, dulling, lifting, sagging, or other such imperfections on the topcoat.

Flash times are clearly indicated on all information sheets and application guides for all paint products. Second and final coats may require longer flash times than initial coats. Read and follow the directions for the paint system employed. They are not all the same. This goes for undercoats, topcoats, and clearcoats.

CLEAR COAT FINISHES

Along with offering better protection for metallics and other paints, clear coats reduce the amount of color material needed for a good finish, thus reducing some of the overall solvent needed and helping manufacturers stay within governmental guidelines. Clear-coat finishes are also good for smoothing out sharp paint lines left behind along custom graphic paint edges. Additionally, painters

Whether you're painting something as small as a gas filler door or as large as a truck bed or complete vehicle, remember to use wax and grease remover before every application of anything in the paint system. This includes sanding, body filler, primer sufacer, sealer, base coat, and clear coat. Then also spray off the entire surface with an air nozzle, to make sure no wax and grease remover or moisture of any kind is left on the surface.

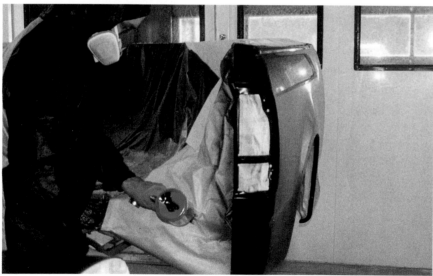

Paint the edges of an area first, then the main surface. That way, overspray helps cover the main area, and you can apply less paint there. If you get the main area painted to the appropriate thickness first, then do the edges, the extra paint from the overspray may cause blemishes on the main surface.

use clear to help feather in repaints along adjacent panels and old paint perimeters.

Applying clear is no different from applying other paints. You have to maintain a close eye on your work, so that each pass is uniform. Exterior body parts, such as door handles and key locks, can be masked for clear paint applications without as much concern about overspray blemishes as with color coats. This is because clear coat dries to a clear, invisible finish. Beware not to spray clear until the last color coat has dried for the recommended period. Spraying clear too early will trap the color coat's solvents and lead to the same finish problems described above.

TRI-STAGE FINISHES

Originally reserved for custom jobs or high-end vehicles, tri-stage paint systems are becoming more common. Whether custom or original, tri-stage finishes include a base coat, color coat, and clear coat. The base coat gives the color coat a compatible base and also influences its appearance. For example, a purple coat sprayed over a silver base will have a different tint than the same color sprayed over a white base.

As you would with any other paint, you apply base coats to cover all intended new paint surfaces. After the recommended flash time has elapsed, spray on color coat using the techniques described earlier. When you've sprayed the correct number of color coats and the proper flash time has passed, proceed to the clearcoat stage. Be sure to clean your spray gun according to the methods described earlier and the paint and spray-gun manufacturers' instructions.

Once the final coat of clear has dried for the recommended period, you'll be able to wet-sand blemishes and buff areas that need extra polishing. The clear-coat finish will prevent wet sanding or polishing from distorting the blended color achieved between the base coat and color coat.

PLASTIC OR FLEXIBLE ASSEMBLIES

A great many different kinds of plastics are in use today on all types of automobile parts and assemblies. They range from acrylonitrile butadiene styrene (ABS) to thermoplastic olefin (TPO) and sheet molded compounds (SMC) to reaction injection molded plastic (RIM). Each has its own place, from rigid grillework sections to flexible bumper covers.

If you're using lacquer or enamel paint, such as on a vintage restoration, any flexible components should be sprayed with paint containing a special additive that allows it to flex along with the part. You may also have to use special undercoats in addition to topcoat additives. The only way to be certain that the products that you use are compatible and designed for painting the parts you intend to spray is to check with your auto body paint and supply specialist. If you're using a base-coat/clear-coat paint system, however, flex additives are no longer necessary because of the flexible characteristics of today's urethane products.

The same caution applies to rigid plastics. Some materials are compatible with normal painting systems, while others may require specific undercoats. By using the designed paint system and proper additives, along with the recommended preparation techniques, you will be assured that newly applied paint coats will not peel, crack, or flake off. In rare cases, you cannot repaint certain solvent-sensitive plastic or urethane parts when the factory primer seal has been broken. In those situations, you have to replace the parts.

AFTER SPRAYING PAINT

Once you've painted the vehicle to your satisfaction, you need to complete several further tasks to ensure the overall quality of the job. Once the paint has dried sufficiently, wet-sand nibs smooth and carefully

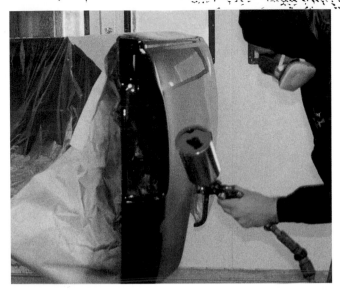

Even when painting the subtle wheelwell flare, position the spray-paint gun so it's perpendicular to the area that bulges slightly from the main panel. The flare varies in width from about 1 to 2 inches wide, so it's not large, but it's still important to apply the paint evenly. Remember that when using a base-coat/clear-coat paint system, the base coat should be applied only to achieve complete coverage. Gloss will come from the clear.

Kneeling helps this painter see where he's applying the clear. Notice how he took the time to mask the inner wheelwell and the inside of the bed of this pickup truck.

remove the masking tape to prevent unnecessary paint-edge peeling or other accidental finish damage. Read the sections on wet sanding and buffing before removing any masking material.

Uncatalyzed enamels cannot withstand wet sanding or polishing. With this kind of paint system,

what you see is what you get, unless you later decide to sand a completely cured but blemished panel down to the substrate and repaint it to perfection.

Certain lacquer and urethane paint finishes can be wet sanded and polished to remove nibs, flatten orange peel, and otherwise smooth small blemishes. This work is normally done on clear coats, as opposed to color coats, and may require additional light applications of clear. For this reason, professionals seldom remove masking material until they're pleased with the entire paint job and are satisfied that they've remedied all imperfections.

DRYING TIMES

Automotive paint has to dry. If not allowed to do so in a clean environment, the wet finish can be contaminated by dust, dirt, or other debris. Professional painters always leave freshly sprayed vehicles in paint booths until enough time has elapsed for the material to cure completely, according to the paint manufacturer's recommendations.

For example, acrylic urethane paints should dry 6–8 hours at 70 degrees Fahrenheit or forced dried for 40 minutes at 140 degrees. Force drying requires portable infrared heaters or high-tech paint booths equipped with heating units. As stressed earlier, proper drying is essential to prevent future coats from being damaged by trapped solvents.

Factory paint jobs with urethane paint products and those that are suitable for force drying are baked on body surfaces at temperatures around 450 degrees

Fahrenheit. This can be accomplished only while cars are stripped. Otherwise, plastic, rubber, and vinyl parts would melt. Cars still equipped with these items cannot be force dried at temperatures above 160 degrees. Excessive heat can also damage the vehicle's computer.

There are other factors to consider when using heat lamps and other force dry methods. Initial flash times are extremely important. Most paint products must air dry for 15 minutes or longer on their own, to let the bulk of the solvent material evaporate. Too much heat too soon will evaporate this solvent too quickly, causing blemishes.

Some paint finishes have a window of time during which you must wet sand or recoat. Wait beyond that period and you may have to scuff sand and clean the surface again before applying touchup coats, to get proper adhesion.

WET SANDING

Confirm ahead of time that the paint system you use is compatible with wet sanding. Your auto body paint and supply jobber can do this while you're discussing your paint needs at the time of purchase. Each automotive paint manufacturer has its own set of guidelines. What may be good for PPG's Deltron system may not be so good for a BASF or DuPont system. In fact, you might even be advised to completely disregard wet sanding and opt instead for polishing to guarantee a perfect finish with the type of product you've chosen.

To ensure good paint adhesion, the freshly washed bedside is scuffed with 400-grit sandpaper. Since a base coat will be applied to approximately half the panel and clearcoat will be applied to all of it, the entire panel must be scuffed. After the panel is scuffed, it will be cleaned again with wax and grease remover and masked completely before it's painted.

Not every type of paint system can be wet sanded. Enamels, for example, cure with a sort of film on their surface, which will be damaged if broken by sandpaper or harsh polish.

Lacquers and some urethane products can be sanded with fine sandpaper soon after they have cured. Although wet-sanding color coats is not recommended, you might be able to lightly sand off nibs, providing you're prepared to touch up the spots with a light color coat. Wet sanding yields its best results on clearcoats that are then polished.

Base-coat/clear-coat paint systems generally call for a number of color coats and then clear coats. Especially with candy finishes, sanding directly on the color surface will distort the tint and cause a visible blemish. Wet sanding for them is done on clear coats only. Your wet sanding efforts should be concentrated on clearcoats, so as not disturb the underlying color coats. Wet sanding clear coats will bring out a much deeper shine and gloss when followed by controlled buffing and polishing.

Painters use very fine 1500 to 2500-grit sandpaper with water to smooth or remove minor blemishes on cured paint finishes designed to allow wet sanding. Only sandpaper designated wet-or-dry should be used. Those that are not waterproof will fall apart.

As with all other sanding tasks, use a sanding block. Since nibs of dirt or dust are small, fold sandpaper around a wooden paint-stir stick instead of using a large hand block. Their 1-inch width is great for smoothing small spots. Use only light pressure for this type of delicate sanding. Be sure to dip sandpaper in a bucket of water frequently, to keep the paint surface wet and reduce the amount of material buildup on the sandpaper. Add a small amount of mild car-washing soap to the water bucket, to provide lubrication to the sandpaper. The sandpaper should also be allowed to soak in water for 15 minutes before wet sanding.

If certain blemished areas need a lot of sanding, you may need to apply new coats of clear. This is why you should leave masking material in place during wet sanding.

In some cases, such as on show cars, the entire car body may be wet sanded to bring out the richest, deepest, and most lustrous shine possible. Because they anticipate extensive wet sanding and polishing operations, painters of these cars make sure they have applied plenty of clear coats.

REMOVING MASKING MATERIAL

To many enthusiastic automobile painters, removing masking paper and tape to reveal a new paint job or quality spot paint repair is like opening birthday presents. It's always a pleasure to see a finished product, especially after viewing it in primer for any length of time. However, unlike the wrapping paper on presents, masking materials must be removed carefully, to prevent finish damage.

As we've discussed, paint has solids in it that build up on car bodies. Especially on jobs where

With the edges covered, the rest of this bedside can be coated with clear. After each coat of clear has had sufficient time to flash, all the dust, dirt, and nibs can be lightly sanded out if necessary prior to the next coat. In collision repairs, two or three coats of clear would typically be applied, with little to no sanding between coats. Custom show-car painters do lots of sanding with extremely fine sandpaper between coats of clear to achieve those mirror-finish paint jobs that cost tens of thousands of dollars. Sanding between clear coats is what makes the difference between a good paint job and a great one. You decide what best suits your needs.

numerous color coats and clear coats were applied, the thickness of the paint can bridge the lips along masking tape edges. What will occur, in some situations, is the formation of a paint film on a car body that continues over to include the top of the tape. If you pull the tape straight up, it could tear flakes of paint from the body surface.

To prevent paint flaking or peeling along the edge of masking tape strips, painters pull tape away from the newly painted body area, as opposed to straight up off the panel, and back upon itself, to create a sharp angle at the point where it leaves the surface. This sharp angle can cut extra-thin paint films, so they don't cause flakes or cracks on the finish.

When they've applied several color and clear coats along a masked edge, meticulous painters often use a sharp razor blade to cut the paint film between the panel surface and tape edge. If you damage the paint while removing the masking material, you'll have to sand and repaint as needed.

RUB OUT AND BUFFING

As with wet sanding, not every type of paint system can stand up to vigorous polishing or rubbing out. With single-stage urethane, for example, buffing with a gritty compound will only dull the surface and ruin the finish. In contrast, polishing a catalyzed urethane (base coat/clear coat) or cured lacquer can make the finishes much more brilliant, lustrous, and deep shining.

A wide variety of polishing compounds is available for new paint finishes. Auto body paint and supply stores carry the largest selection. Some are designed to be used by hand, while others can safely be polished with buffing machines. Foam pads work best with prescribed compounds and buffing machines limited to slower rpm, while pads made with cloth are better suited for other compounds and machine speeds. Be sure to get what is appropriate for your paint.

Basically, rubbing compounds include relatively coarse polishing grit material. They are designed to quickly remove blemishes and flatten paint finishes. Because these compounds contain grit, they leave behind light scratches or swirls. Therefore, after using compound to flatten orange peel or produce a higher surface luster, you'll need to buff or polish the paint finish with a fine grit material. This may involve, especially with dark colors, exceptionally soft-finish buffing pads and wax.

As refinish products have changed over the years, some ideas that seem like common sense are no longer valid. Manufacturers of the new urethane paint products often suggest polishing with 2,000-grit compound using a foam pad. This should minimize swirls and yield a satisfactory finish the first time around. If swirls are still present, you should go back to a slightly coarser compound to remove the swirls, then use the finer 2,000-grit again. With older technology, painters would start

With the body repaired, this pickup truck is moved to the paint preparation area. Primer sufacer has been applied to about the rear third of the bedside. To blend the color, a base coat will be applied from the very rear edge to about the front of the wheelwell, with full coverage centering over the repaired area and feathering out from there. Clear coat will cover the entire bedside to further blend the repaired area into the old.

with the coarse rubbing compound, then work up to the finer stuff, instead of this seemingly backward procedure.

Although paint finishes may appear dry, especially those that included a hardening agent, they may not be ready for buffing right away. Allow sufficient time for all solvents to evaporate before smothering them with polishing compound. Application guides and information sheets generally list the recommended time.

By hand, use a soft, clean cloth for rubbing out and polishing, and follow directions on the product label. Many auto enthusiasts apply polish in straight back-and-forth movements from the front to back of vehicles, instead of circular patterns. They profess that polishing panels in this manner greatly reduces their chances for creating swirls.

You need experience practicing with a buffing machine before using it on your car's new paint job. Practicing will help you avoid a paint burn—polishing through the paint finish down to primer or bare metal. Buffers with maximum speeds of about 1,450 rpm are best for novices. Machines with faster revolutions require more experience. Be aware that even the slower, 1,450-rpm buffers are quite capable of causing paint burns if you don't pay close attention to what you're doing.

To use a buffer, first spread out a few strips of compound parallel to the floor, about 4–6 inches apart. Cover an area no bigger than 2 square feet.

Operate the buffing pad on top of a compound strip and work it over that strip's area, gradually moving down to pick up successive strips. The idea is to buff a 2-square-foot area while not allowing the pad to run dry of compound. Keep buffing on that body section until compound is gone and all that remains is shiny paint.

Buffing pads can be operated back and forth as well as up and down. Always keep them moving. Just as with power sanders, a buffer left in one spot can rub through the paint. Be exceptionally careful buffing near ridges, gaps, and corners. If you hit those surfaces with the buffer, all the buffing force is expended on a small, focused area and will quickly burn through the paint. Instead of running the buffing pad on top of ridges, run it just up to their edge and stop. Some painters prefer to mask edges, ridges, and corners with strips of masking tape, to protect them against accidental buffing burns, then remove the tape and buff them by hand. This might be a good idea for the novice.

If you have to buff in tight areas, such as near door handles, throttle the machine on and off to lower the rpm speed. Slowing the pad in this way will help reduce the possibility of paint burns. Be sure plenty of compound is spread over the area. For extra-confined spaces, apply compound by hand with a soft, damp cloth.

Make sure you don't drag power cords for electric buffers and air hoses for pneumatic models over the

paint finish. A good way to keep them under control while buffing roofs, hoods, and trunk lids is to drape them over your shoulder. To prevent buckles, zippers, snaps, or rivets on your clothing from scratching the car as you move alongside it, wear an apron. A long sweatshirt may also work. If possible, simply avoid clothing with these hard, sharp features.

Power buffers will throw spots of compound all over your car, clothes, and nearby surfaces. Be prepared for this kind of mess by covering adjacent cabinets or workbench items with tarps or dropcloths. Always wipe buffing compound thrown by the buffer off the paint as soon as possible because it can damage the new paint if it's allowed to dry.

As cloth buffing pads become covered with compound, or every three passes, whichever comes first, use a pad spur to clean them. With the pad spinning, gently but securely push a spur into the pad's nap. This will break loose compound and force it out of the pad. You'll be surprised at how much material comes off pads, so be sure to do your pad cleaning away from your car and anything else that you don't want covered with compound or pad lint. You can't clean the buffing pads too much.

OVERSPRAY

Polishing and buffing efforts usually work well to remove light traces of overspray from hoods, roofs, and trunk lids. Extra-heavy overspray residue may require a strong polishing compound for complete removal. For severe problems, consult your auto body paint and supply jobber.

If epoxy primer has been applied to keep moisture from penetrating through to the metal surface below, parts may be wet sanded to achieve the ultimate in smoothness before spraying color coats and clear. You can also wet-sand painted parts. (The paint serves as a sealer to keep moisture from the metal below.) Using progressively finer sandpaper, 1500 to 2500 grit, soaked in water, and sand in a circular motion, using light pressure on the sanding block. A slight amount of car-washing soap added to the water lubricates the sandpaper. It is critical not to sand through the paint.

If you've been meticulous with your masking, most overspray problems, if any, will involve items like tailpipes, fenderwells, horn units, and other lowdown pieces. You could spend a lot of time removing overspray from painted items, like fenderwells, or spend a lot less by simply covering overspray with black paint or undercoat. If this won't work for some reason, such as a show car with matching-color fenderwells, you'll have to sand, polish, or possibly even repaint affected areas.

Overspray on chrome might be easily removed with a chrome polish. Heavy concentrations may require number 0000 steel wool with polish. Chrome items commonly prone to overspray include tailpipes, wheels, bumpers, grille pieces, and trim. The best way to avoid overspray problems on these accessories is to mask them properly, with plenty of tape to secure paper edges, so puffs of paint spray can't infiltrate the masked space.

Remove paint overspray from glass using the solvent appropriate to the vehicle's paint system. Dab some solvent on a clean cloth and rub off overspray. If that doesn't work, try using number 0000 or finer steel wool and solvent. (**Caution:** Some newer windshields are made with acrylic ingredients that even fine steel wool may scratch. If you aren't sure whether your car's windshield is solid glass or acrylic, check with a dealership service department, auto glass business, or your auto body paint and supply jobber.) In extreme cases, you might have to use a razor blade and a delicate touch to scrape overspray off glass.

the CLEARING GAME

BY CRAIG FRASER

In the custom painting field, there's probably nothing less appreciated and yet as important as the clear coat. Clear coating is not just a good idea—it's a necessity. Since 99 percent of all show-quality graphic jobs are two-stage base-coat urethanes, it's a safe bet that after the artwork is done, the final piece is clear coated. While many people may not consider spraying clear to be an art form, after trying to clear coat something yourself, your attitude will change. There is a phrase in the industry: "Behind every good clear coater, there's a better buffer." Though this may be true in some circles, clear coating remains an art form that is easily completed, yet rarely mastered.

This chapter focuses on urethane clear coating. Although there are a number of synthetic enamel, lacquer-based, and even water-based urethane clears floating around, the bad boys on the block are the solvent-based polymers, known as acrylic urethanes and urethane enamels. Recent urethanes are taking advantage of the most current innovations in polymer technology.

Even though the clear may be fresh from the can, it's a good practice to run all material through a strainer before spraying. All it takes is one blotch of hardened resin to ruin your day. Also be sure to keep the cans sealed tight. Besides being the law, it prevents the clear from becoming contaminated by water vapor, which can cause urea crystals to form.

WHAT IS CLEAR?

In automotive painting, a clear coat is a protective coating sprayed over the base coat. This not only protects and seals the paint from the elements, but gives the final paint job its overall gloss and deep shine. All automotive final clear coats are categorized as catalyzed clear. In the acrylic urethane field, these clears use an isocyanate-based catalyst to harden the clear much like the catalyst in epoxy cement hardens the resin. When the catalyst is mixed with the urethane resins and reducing solvents, the chemical reaction causes heat, a necessary ingredient in the drying process. While all urethanes are toxic and require proper ventilation as well as respirators, isocyanates are the main bad guys out there. Isocyanates are a nerve toxin and require the use of professional respirators at all times. For complete protection from long-term exposure, the Occupational Health and Safety Administration (OSHA) recommends using fresh-air systems in the work environment whenever isocyanates are present.

The base coat is the first stage of the two-stage system and the clear coat is the second. Single-stage paint, used for single-color paint jobs, is any paint that has the clear already mixed in. A three- or four-stage system is used to describe a job that requires additional clear coats—these either contain a mica-based pearlescence, an applied kandy, or a tinted clear that is shot over an existing metallic and then sprayed with a final coat of transparent clear to finish the job. The easiest way to spot multiple-stage paint jobs is by the illusion of depth in the color created by the number of coats of transparent kandies or clear coats. The more layers of clear painted on a surface, the better the ability of the paint to trap, reflect, and amplify light. Metallic bases, metal flakes, and pearls can be added to give the clear coat the ability to modify light. Because of the hardened resins and the high DOI factor (Distinctness of Image), urethane clears can be buffed and polished to a mirror-like finish, unlike the older modified alkyd enamel systems that, while sufficient at the time, had yellowing problems. Urethane clears are not only handy in the automotive field, but also when painting on guitars and other hard surfaces like carbon fiber, fiberglass, and even floors. Due to their flexible nature and UV-absorbing factor, they've been experimented with on urethanes vinyl substrates as a sealer and as protective coating for airbrushed effects on vinyl.

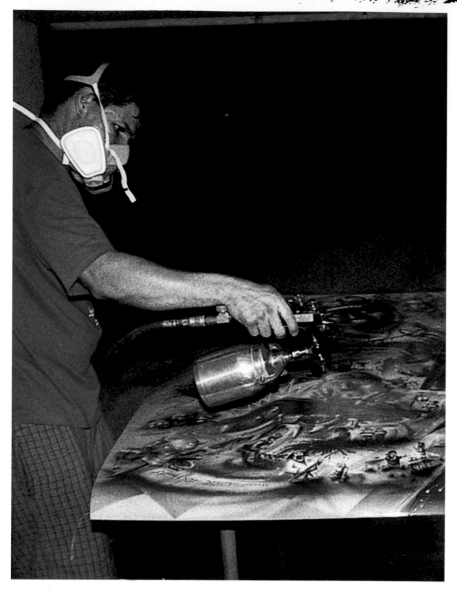

When clear coating a graphic job or hood mural, Dion chooses between his gravity-feed airbrush and his siphon-feed setup. Here he's using the siphon-feed, since he wants less material sprayed when laying the first wet coat on the hood. The gravity-feed has a higher flow rate and has a better reach for rooflines and under doorsills.

HVLP AND OTHER ACRONYMS

The weapon of choice for today's hot-shot clear coaters is the HVLP (High Volume Low Pressure) gun. These guns put out a higher volume of material with less overall nozzle pressure, resulting in less overspray waste and more material on the surface. Not only are they more environmentally friendly, but they have also improved spray quality. Able to hold a wider, more even fan of material (up to 17 inches in some cases), these guns have a material-transfer percentage of anywhere from 70- to 90-percent compared to the 20- to 30-percent efficiency of the older siphon-feed, non-HVLP models. HVLP spray guns come in both siphon-feed and gravity-feed models. Many professional painters prefer the gravity-feed spray guns to the siphon, due to the higher-volume rate of flow and the added clearance under the gun (the color cup is mounted on top which makes shooting car roofs a lot easier on the wrists). The automotive spray gun, though appearing unchanged on its surface, has undergone more internal design changes in the last five years than it has in the last five decades. The number of gun manufacturers has increased as well. As with many of the top-of-the-line paints, which one is best is a matter of personal preference. But remember, the gun doesn't make the artist, it just makes his job easier.

CLEARLY SPEAKING

In light of today's advanced chemical technology and improved urethane clear coats, you would think that clear coating would become simpler, as well as better. In actuality, it's becoming more complicated. With the advanced chemicals being developed to better catalyze and dry the clears, the clearing process is becoming more of a thinking person's game, rather than just something you spray out of your paint gun. Clear coaters must now learn more about chemicals and reactive properties to understand the modified mixing ratios required and environments needed for the best clear coats. Safety precautions are becoming more complicated as well. Clear coats may be environmentally safer now, but they're more dangerous for people. In order to better understand this process, take one of the classes or workshops that individual paint manufacturers offer to accredit painters for their paint lines. Besides catalyzed clears, there are a whole batch of air-dry clears that have become known as intercoats. These intermediary clears are distant cousins to the old air-dry lacquers and are designed to be sprayed on between colors to protect from color bleeds and promoted adhesion, or act as a fast-drying carrier for a pearl or kandy tint. Being air-dry, these interclears are still urethane based and still require solvent for reducing, but since there's no catalyst involved they don't have the structural integrity of the catalyzed clears and cannot be used as a topcoat. Because of their nonstructural strength, it's actually a good idea to limit the number of coats to four when spraying with them. Otherwise, there could be adhesion problems as well as cracking.

While there are a number of books and paint articles defining the art of painting and clearing, probably the best advice is to experiment. Most clears that are illegal in your area will be unavailable; and as far as mixing ratios go, labeling is usually pretty self-explanatory. For example, since temperature is a major variable, the clear coater's use of the proper reducer, as well as the proper amount, can have a great effect on the final finish of the piece. Take into account that the pressure at the gun, the possible use of an accelerator to increase drying, and the window between wet coats are all situations that can be followed in the instructions, but need to be experienced first-hand to be truly enjoyed.

To sum up, find an accomplished painter and pick his brain, which is why the first piece of equipment in your shop should be a telephone.

YES, GRASSHOPPER

Pete "when-you-can-take-this-paint-gun-from-my-hand, it-will-be-time-for-you-to-leave" Santini of Santini Paint of Westminster, California, is one of today's masters of clear coating. He's been in the trenches as a second-generation car painter and kustomizer and takes a practical approach to painting.

Though hand cleaning is probably the most effective method, it is also time consuming. No paint shop should be without a gun washer. This is a top-gun model that uses air-powered cleaning solvent to spray on and through the guns.

"Pick up a gun and start spraying," Pete suggests. "You can only learn so much from the tech manuals and seminars. You've gotta just get in the booth and start spraying. Until then, it's all academic. And it's not just a 9-to-5 job. You've got to be willing to stay the extra time to learn. When you're working, you can't expect the boss to let you stand around and watch. When you go to college, no one pays you to learn, and it's the same way in the paint booth. The real learning takes place at 11:00 at night when you have a problem, you can't reclear it tomorrow, and you've got to make a decision."

Pete prefers to use a gravity-feed HVLP gun due to the higher volume of material it can move. "Today's guns not only spray more efficiently, but the higher atomization of the clear makes the new guns work better with today's clears. With the new clears having

Whenever enamel pinstriping is involved, it's important to catalyze the enamel striping paint with the same catalyst being used in the urethane clear. Otherwise the clear can reactivate the enamel and cause lifting, as well as ribboning, in the pinstripe.

such a high solids content [the amount of actual urethane resins that ends up in the finished clear coat], you don't need to bury the work with multiple coats. Actually, too much of the new clears can end up giving a milky consistency to the finish."

According to Pete, there are currently problems in the industry. "It's a toss-up between the number of new products being thrown out on the market and the cost of materials today. When a major paint manufacturer has five new clears come out within three to five yearsit makes it tough for painters.

This problem is quite common in the industry, but can be seen as a direct result of competition between paint companies to put out the best product first. In defense of the paint companies, it's also a direct

result of the constant changes in the environmental laws in a given area. While these laws do protect the environment, the bureaucracy has pushed the paint costs to the point of bankruptcy for many painters.

"The average amount of materials to primer, paint, and clear a Camaro today run as high as $900. That same car would have cost less than $400 five years ago, the increase being in the paint and the clear. The profit has got to come from the labor now. There's no room for profit in the materials for the painter," according to Pete.

The talents of a truly gifted clear coater are not necessarily seen in the end product; a good buffer can fix runs, sags, and an orange peel in the clear. A talented clear coater saves not only materials but time

Clear coats look better with a little buffing and polishing.

by keeping these problems to a minimum. In an industry where labor and design innovation are the only profit center, only the talented can survive.

In addition to books and articles, videos are also available for automotive painters. Everyone should try clear coating at least once, but for quality of finish and profit, hire a professional. Even if you have an in-house clear coater, picking up a gun and spraying will give you an appreciation for the art and eventually make you a better automotive painter or airbrusher.

CHAPTER

3.1

FLAMING

BY CRAIG FRASER

Since the first custom hit the streets, the flame job has been the ultimate poster child of the hot-rod era. While there are a number of ways to do a flame job correctly, there are just as many ways to do a flame job badly. For that reason, there have been entire books written on the subject.

Flames are somewhat misleading. The trick to flames is to realize that they must occupy negative and positive space simultaneously in order to balance out the design. In other words, the flames should appear as flames in the positive sense, but in the negative space they should resemble drips. If the drips don't appear balanced, aren't symmetrical, or don't look like drips at all, then your flames are going to suffer as well. The design should also have continuity. Look at the flame in this demo as if it were a body. There's a neck, then a torso, and then two final licks coming out of the top, which

could become the neck of a continuing flame. Like juggling, it's a lot easier to demonstrate than to describe.

MATERIALS & EQUIPMENT

3/4-inch masking tape
1/8-inch blue fineline vinyl tape
Scouring pad
X-acto knife
Black, hot pink, violet paint
Precleaner
Clear coat
Green, lemon yellow striping urethane
Reducer
#000 sword striper
Touch-up gun
Bottle-feed airbrush
Freehand shield

STEP 1

Using a scouring pad, scuff a powder-coated sign blank. On an actual vehicle, if a paint job is fresh enough, you can use the pads for total prepping, but 600-grit wet/dry sandpaper is recommended because it does a more thorough job.

STEP 2

Using blue fineline vinyl tape, begin laying out the general pattern of the flames. Working from left to right, focus on the even balance between the body and the licks, or tongues, of the flames. Keep an eye on the negative and positive space to balance the overall design on the board, as well as on the flames themselves.

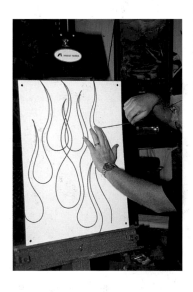

STEP 3

When using blue fineline vinyl tape, you must work both hands in unison to pull and place the design. This tape is pressure-sensitive, and while it's repositionable, you can burnish it down to increase the adhesion. Make sure to press especially hard on the ends where they overlap to prevent paint bleeding.

STEP 4

With a roll of 3/4-inch masking tape, begin masking off the flames, butting the tape against the blue fineline vinyl tape. Be sure not to leave any gaps that can allow paint to work its way under the tape.

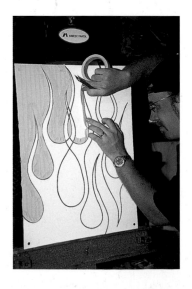

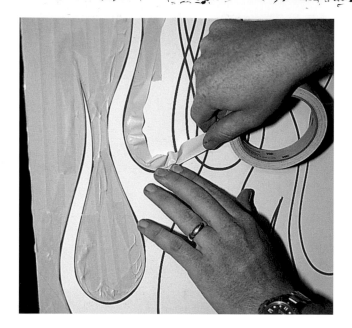

STEP 5

The tape can roll on an inside curve, but not an outside curve. By spinning the tape around the design, you can mask the flames off quickly without having to cut different sections out. It's important to press the folds down, since they can channel the overspray to the masked-off areas like little tunnels.

STEP 6

Using an X-acto knife, cut out the overlapping areas of the blue fineline vinyl tape. (The crossover section of the flame will be sprayed with the rest of the design and the overlap will be drop shadowed later with the airbrush.)

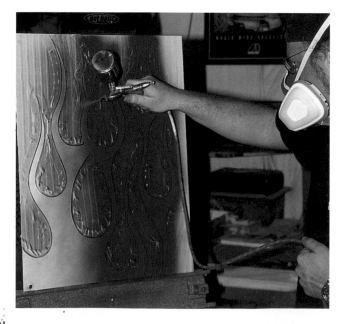

STEP 7

Mix a batch of hot pink paint and use the touch-up airbrush to spray the design. On a full-size vehicle, a larger gun would be better, but for this panel and small helmets or tanks, the touch-up gun is just the right size.

STEP 8

Using a mixture of violet and clear, spray the fades onto the tips. Use the freehand shield to help create the weaving effect of the flames while you drop-shadow the corresponding licks. The clear coat not only improves the flow of the paint, but also acts as a structural binder to the violet toner.

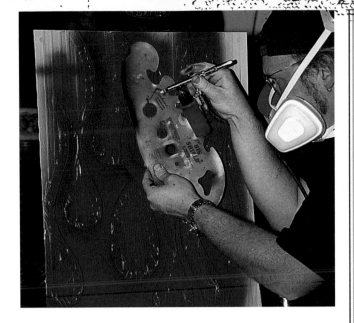

STEP 9

Being careful not to peel the paint, remove the masking from the design. Always pull the tape back against itself. This will prevent the tape from lifting and chipping along the tape edge.

STEP 10

Using a dry scouring pad, scuff off any tape residue and eliminate any overspray that may have snuck through the tape. A little precleaner on a damp towel can also help with this.

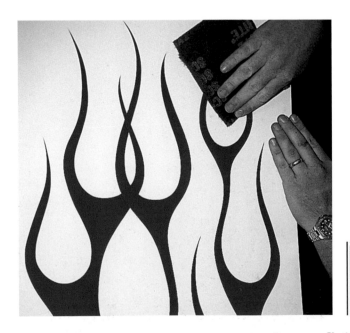

STEP 11

With the bottle-feed airbrush, mix up a batch of
transparent black and lay in the drop shadow of the
flame. Create the transparent black by over-reducing the
paint. Masking isn't necessary since the transparent
black won't discolor the flames too much.

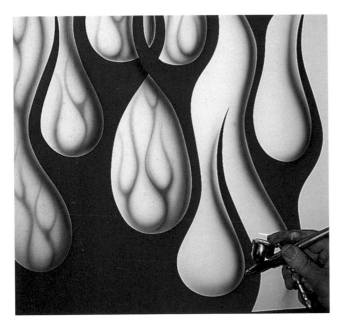

STEP 12

To fill in some space, use the transparent violet to
airbrush in some freehand flames. This not only looks
good, but it's a great way to hide any imperfections
that you couldn't eliminate with the scouring pad.

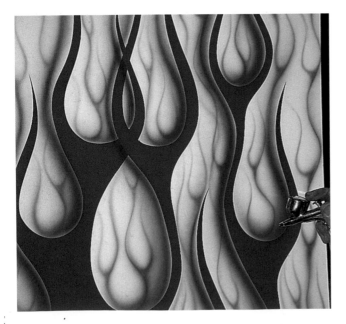

STEP 13

Use the violet to go back over the drop shadows too.
Remember, always think on your feet when painting. If
something doesn't look right, fix it instead of hoping no
one will notice it!

STEP 14

Before pinstriping, wipe the entire surface down with a little precleaner. You can use any precleaner to remove overspray or tape residue—just be sure it's not too strong or it will take off all your fades and freehand flames.

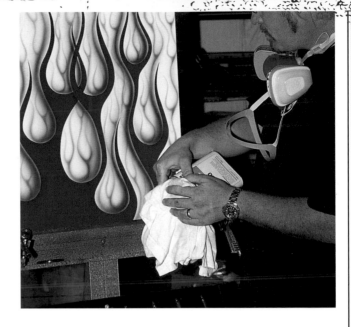

STEP 15

Mix a batch of lime green striping urethane by combining green and a small amount of lemon yellow. Carefully pinstripe the outside edge of the flame with a #000 (sword) striper brush. If this were an actual car, you would clear coat the flames first and then pinstripe the flames between clear coats. This buries the edge of the flame so that it doesn't peek through the pinstripe. Pinstriping designs on small panels is a great way to build up your pinstriping chops on small, manageable projects.

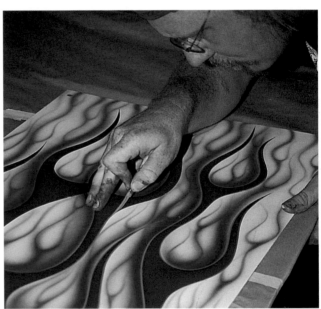

STEP 16

And now your flame job is just itching to be put on a street rod. Practicing is the only way to pick up this technique. And remember, there's no correct style. If you like it, the paint doesn't fall off, and small children don't cry when they see it, then you've done your job.

tribal FLAMES

BY CRAIG FRASER

Tribal graphics have been getting a lot of attention lately, especially the tribal flame design—a hybrid of the classic flame and tribal patterning. This design became popular with the resurgence of the flame job and the popularity of tribal tattooing. Tattoos and tattoo flash art have always been a good source of inspiration for automotive graphics, and vice-versa. Kick this fairly simple design up a notch with a little lizard skin airbrushing. Any graphic can be souped-up with this type of airbrushing. You'll see.

MATERIALS & EQUIPMENT
Masking tape
1/8-inch blue fineline vinyl tape
Transfer paper
Scouring pad
X-acto knife
Plastic wrap
Black, light blue paint
Post sanding cleaner
Precleaner
Lime green pearl paint
Green candy base coat
Dry pearl
Marblizer
Hot pink paint
Violet paint
Clear coat
Green and yellow striping urethane
Light blue and white striping urethane
Reducer
#000 sword striper
Top-feed airbrush
Touch-up gun
Bottle-feed airbrush
Freehand shield

STEP 1
Paint the sign blank black to show the flame design over a darker surface, and mask the border with masking tape. This isn't necessary for the flame design, but looks nice for a presentation piece. It also gives continuity to your demos, in case you're following along and creating a portfolio.

STEP 2
Lay out the initial flame design using blue fineline vinyl tape. This step is the same as laying out an ordinary set of flames. It's much easier to lay out the standard classical design of the flames, instead of adding the tribal licks first. Since you're going to add the tribal licks and spikes, make the flames a little more open and spaced farther apart.

STEP 3
After the flames are laid out, burnish the tape down to keep it from creeping back and begin adding in the licks and tongues of the tribal patterns. For now, stick to a conservative Polynesian pattern to keep the design less busy. After you get used to the tribal patterning, you can go wild. The vinyl tape is very handy for this, since it's repositionable, allowing you to make a lot of layout mistakes without wasting tape.

STEP 4
With an X-acto knife, remove all the tape overlaps. It's important to realize that the inside of the tapeline is what you're trying to keep clean, not the outside edge. Cut into the original flame to allow the added lick to become a part of the flame body.

STEP 5
In the previous flame demo, you learned how to mask out the flames in the traditional way using 3/4-inch masking tape and paper. For this design, you'll use another technique that is good to use on large, flat areas where there are little or no curves. Using some transfer paper, which is used for transferring vinyl lettering, roll and flatten out the transfer tape onto the surface. By rolling and pulling, you can apply the paper with little or no bubbles. The transfer paper is much like contact paper, but less adhesive.

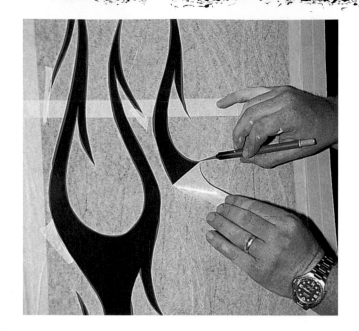

STEP 6

With the X-acto knife, follow the underlying blue tape (you can see it easily through the paper). Carefully cut through the paper, using the blue tape as a buffer to the metal surface. Make sure you don't cut through the paper and tape into the metal surface. This mistake would allow a ghost line to bleed through, possibly damaging the underlying surface, which can cause problems when clear coating.

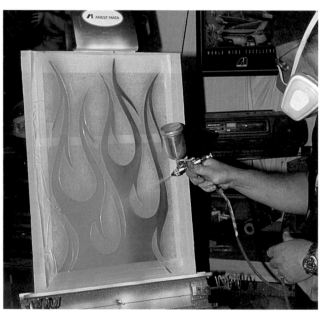

STEP 7

Using the touch-up gun with the fan tip, spray an even coat of lime green pearl paint. The benefit of designer pearl paints is that the metallic/pearl within the base coat gives the paint a high level of opacity and covers very well, as you can see over the black. For this same reason, they don't work well for spraying details later on, as the opaque overspray is devastating to the details of a design.

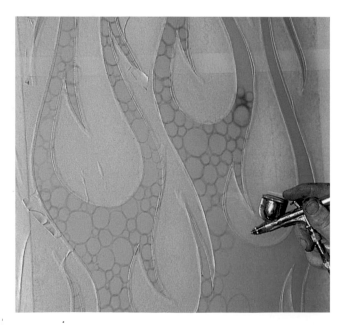

STEP 8

With a top-feed airbrush, mix up a batch of green candy base coat. This candy is very transparent, which allows you to build up layers, steadily increasing the detail, depth, and darkness of the design. The snakeskin is a conglomeration of differing sizes of circles, intertwined within one another. Although labor intensive to apply, it is definitely a unique space filler for graphics.

STEP 9

After sketching in the faint design, go back over the
flames and darken the design, adding shading and
shadowing between the circles to emphasize the texture
and add depth. Use the same transparent kandy green,
just apply it more heavily. The sign of a true candy is
the color's ability to turn almost black when applied
in multiple layers.

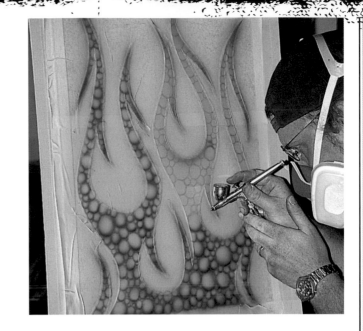

STEP 10

For the final layer, shadow the undersides of the
circles to give them individual depth and a slight
3-D appearance. This gives the snakeskin the illusion
of having a pebbled surface. To bunch out the larger
circles, add a drop of black in the green to speed up
the layering process (but not enough black to kill
the hue).

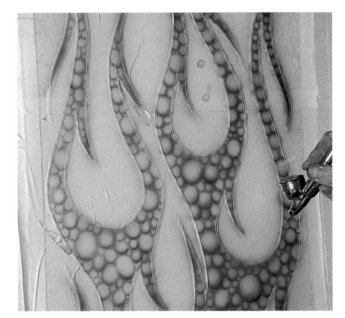

STEP 11

Give the paint an hour to set and then pull off the
tape slowly. Carefully pull back to prevent the paint
from lifting. By pulling the tape back against itself,
you create a knife-type edge that cuts the paint as you
pull, instead of chipping and lifting the paint.
Another nice thing about the transfer tape is that you
can usually lift the entire masking system with one
careful pull (which is a lot better than pulling for a
few hours).

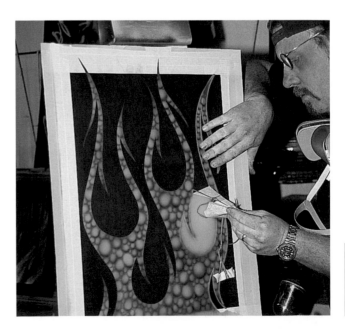

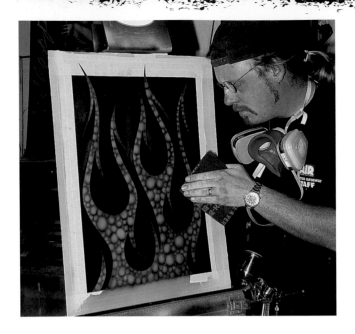

STEP 12

Even the most careful of maskers have problems with blowouts and bleed-throughs. The difference between good painters and bad ones is not in how few mistakes they make, but in how they repair the problems. In this case, use a little piece of scouring pad to scuff off the blow-throughs. Sometimes a rag with a bit of precleaner is all that's necessary to wipe off these annoying overspray demons.

STEP 13

Using light blue paint, begin striping the border edge with a standard #000 sword striper and add a panel effect to the flames. A phone book can be used as a palette for the striper to work the paint into the brush. This gives a constant line and, when working on a vehicle, allows you to pull a solid line down an entire length of a car. Marblizer is a substrate or binding medium that is used as a carrier of dry pearl. It dries slowly, which gives you time to manipulate the surface of the sprayed area.

STEP 14

Though you can use anything to manipulate the surface, try to use the classic "old school" technique of plastic wrap. While the marblizer is still wet, place the plastic wrap on the surface. The plastic wrap gives an effect similar to that of veins in marble. The effects can vary, depending on the amount of time the plastic is on the surface, or if it is shifted on the surface. If there's a problem with the surface texture, re-spray the area with marblizer, which will reactivate the surface and allow you to create another effect.

STEP 15

Add a small teaspoon of dry pearl to some transparent marblizer.

STEP 16

Allow the marblizer about half an hour to dry, then spray the entire surface with a protective layer of clear. Remove the masking and the piece is ready to be pinstriped. The protective clear is necessary if you have to wipe the pinstriping off without damaging the underlying design. Combine light blue and white striping urethanes and begin striping the flame.

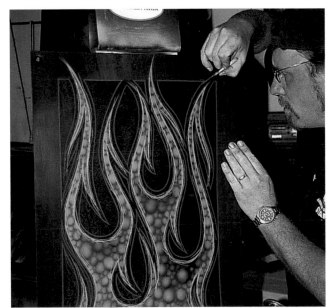

STEP 17

This is a good example of a tribal flame with a little bit of the old school patterning and some airbrushed goodies. Knowing how to modify a flame design to meet your needs will give you a competitive edge and make your designs stand out as your own.

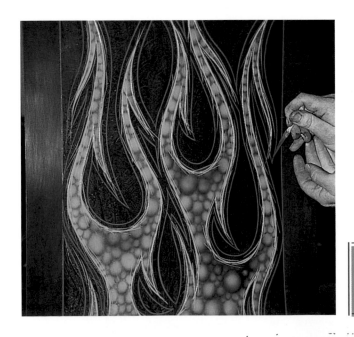

carbon FIBER tribal

BY CRAIG FRASER

A new graphic style to keep an eye on is "stylized" tribal designs. Used for over a thousand years in Polynesian religious art, in Celtic art of the medieval period, and in contemporary culture as tattoos, this style has recently increased in popularity among graphic painters. During the past few years, the new trends in customs have started to resemble some of the popular styles used for tattoos. With tattooing and custom painting at an all-time high, it makes sense that the two fields would influence each other.

In this demo, an airbrush effect was incorporated into the tribal graphic by using airbrush and an adhesive stencil system.

MATERIALS & EQUIPMENT

3/4-inch masking tape
Blue fineline vinyl tape
Transparent transfer tape
X-acto knife
Plastic vinyl squeegee
Drywall grid repair tape (adhesive-backed)
Precleaner
Black base coat
Tangerine candy, root beer candy
Reducer
Gold and orange dry pearl
Gold striping urethane
#000 sword striper
Top-feed airbrush
Touch-up gun

STEP 1

Mask a standard white sign blank using 3/4-inch masking tape to create a border for the design. The border will also give you some leeway in case the edge needs to be trimmed after dings and drops.

STEP 2

Begin laying out the tribal pattern with blue fineline vinyl tape. This particular pattern is along the lines of a stylized Polynesian tattoo. If you were to make it more symmetrical and add a few crossover knotting designs, it would have more of a Celtic look. Some people like to lay down transfer paper and draw the pattern out with pencil, but the freehand tape method will make the design look more natural and less organized and rigid. This is important to retain the organic nature of the tribal pattern (and saves a lot of time in the long run).

STEP 3

When the design layout is complete, use an X-acto knife to carefully cut away any excess overlaps within the design. If you like, you can add a floating circle in the design, as was done here. This is not necessarily a true tribal style, but it does add to the balance of the piece and mimics a little of the yin-yang motif.

STEP 4

Instead of using 3/4-inch tape (which would be a nightmare), lay transparent transfer tape over the entire piece and then cut it out with the X-acto knife. Use the vinyl squeegee to smooth out the transfer paper and eliminate any bubbles that can lead to paint bleeds.

STEP 5

Normally, it would not be wise to use an X-acto knife to cut out an entire design, but with the blue tape acting as a surface buffer, there's little chance of scoring the underlying paint. But be careful—a cut through the blue tape can cause a nasty paint bleed.

STEP 6

To achieve the carbon fiber color, use a black metallic base, almost gunmetal grey. Add a little graphite pearl to the black base coat to create the color. When adding the dry pearl, add small quantities at a time and to mix the paint thoroughly. If you add too much at one time, the paint will clog your airbrush and cause spitting.

STEP 7

Since you want the pearl to be very heavy, bypass the airbrush and go directly to the mini spray gun. Using the fan-tipped gun, spray the entire piece with a standard vertical and horizontal spray pattern. This will give an even surface without any streaks.

STEP 8

Give the paint half an hour to dry, then begin laying in the carbon fiber stencil for the second color. The carbon fiber stencil is a good example of borrowing something from a completely separate industry and using it in airbrushing. The sticky back of the drywall repair tape is perfect for positioning on the surface, and it easily matches up along the edges for laying out larger areas.

STEP 9

When the drywall repair tape is positioned, quickly rub and burnish all the paintable areas. When using a stencil, contact with the surface is important to prevent paint bleeds and overspray. And with a stencil surface as fine and defined as this one, a little overspray can ruin the entire effect.

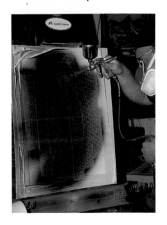

STEP 10

Mix a combination of black base coat with a touch of tangerine candy, root beer candy, and a lot of gold pearl. Spray over the stencil to apply the primary color to the carbon fiber (the black pearl will be the grid of carbon fiber).

STEP 11

Give the paint a few minutes to set, then peel off the drywall tape stencils to reveal the carbon fiber. Remove any adhesive and overspray from the design with a damp rag of precleaner. This will provide a wet look with which to judge the final effect.

STEP 12

Unmask the rest of the design by pulling the tape back against itself to prevent peeling. While adhesion is definitely important, just remember that when the clear coat is applied, even a graphic with the worst adhesion will be anchored down.

STEP 13

With a pure black base coat (a little over-reduced to make it highly transparent), begin spraying in the drop shadows. This really punches out the piece and gives an added 3-D "floating" effect.

STEP 14

For added definition to your tribal effect, create a background texture. The tribal graphic can contrast and play off this symmetrical pattern, creating additional detail and depth.

STEP 15

The final step is the pinstripe. Using your #000 sword striper, carefully pinstripe the tribal edge with gold striping urethane.

This classic tribal tattoo pattern with a carbon fiber twist might be an acquired taste, but it's one of the hottest trends in the custom-paint industry today. Whether you combine it with a conservative graphics scheme or use it as the primary style of an entire paint job, the tribal patterns and Celtic knot designs are definitely hitting.

HOT ROD
striping

BY CRAIG FRASER

Many great effects or techniques began life as accidents. Deadline pressure often forces artists to repair or change direction in a design when a mistake is made. These mishaps become the foundation for countless custom tricks and techniques. The original decorative swirly-Q stripes that Von Dutch pioneered were reportedly first used to hide some grinder marks that were showing through the paint on the hood of a car.

As for striping, the artistic design work of the hot rod industry is some of the most interesting, particularly the edgy pinstripe designs that have been labeled "Von Dutching." Whether it's the artwork of Jimmy C, Von Dutch, Ed Roth, Bob Spena, Bob Bond, Von Franco, or any other striping guru, these freeform designs are the heart of the custom culture. For this reason, this example incorporates their striping styles, a character (much like Dutch's Harvey Shaken), along with some slash striping.

MATERIALS & EQUIPMENT

Scouring pad
Small plastic vinyl squeegee
X-acto knife
Silver/white marblizer
Purple candy
Clear coat
Lemon yellow, green, red, white striping urethane
Lettering quill
#00 sword striper
Touch-up spray gun
Airbrush
Precleaner
Blue fineline masking tape
Automask
Plastic wrap
Chalk

STEP 1

Scuff the surface of a powder-coated aluminum sign blank with a scouring pad. This gives the surface a good tooth for the striping paint (and later clear coat) to stick to. If clear coat is going to be applied, stripe right over the surface. After the surface is scuffed, wipe the dust off using a little precleaner, to prepare the surface for the paint.

STEP 2

To start the piece, mask off and spray a graphic that can then be pinstriped (use a little spraying and airbrushing in the design if you want). Using some blue fineline vinyl tape, lay out a spade inner design, with the outside edge turning into flames. Keep that hot rod retro theme going!

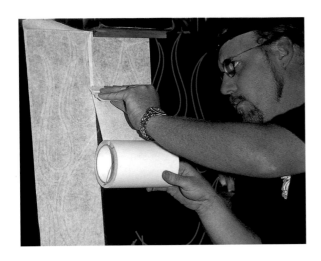

STEP 3

To mask off the tape layout, grab some automask. This material not only cuts more easily than masking tape, but it is also more transparent, so you can see the underlying design. Best of all, it's cheaper for masking large areas. When laying the masking down, you will need a vinyl squeegee to get all the air bubbles out. Small rolls are easier to work with, as you end up with fewer wrinkles when applying it.

STEP 4

With an X-acto knife, cut out the design using the underlying blue tape as a guide. The tape also acts as a buffer to keep the blade from cutting into the base. Be sure to use a sharp blade when cutting tape. A dull blade is more likely to damage and score the underlying surface.

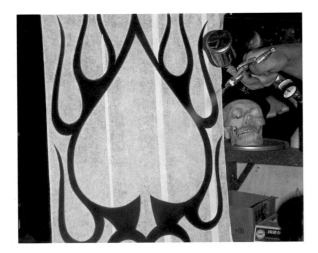

STEP 5

Instead of paint, use a little silver/white marblizer. Using the touch-up gun, spray an even wet coat of marblizer over the exposed surface. With a little stirring, the marblizer is ready to spray right from the can; there's no need for reducer. Marblizer works best over a dark surface. If you use it on any shade lighter than black, you can barely notice the pearlescent effect.

STEP 6

While the marblizer is still wet, apply some plastic wrap. Any type of material can be used for this "ragging" effect, but the thinness of the plastic wrap creates more wrinkles. The way the plastic is applied and removed has a significant effect on the finished product.

STEP 7

Leave the wrap on until the marblizer sets. Then, when it's removed, it rips a little of the marblizer off, giving the design an interesting look. If you remove the plastic when the marblizer is still wet, lift it with care to avoid damaging your masterpiece.

STEP 8

After letting the marblizer dry completely, use an airbrush to fade in some purple kandy. I add the candy to clear to create a base coat kandy. The candy paint gives the marblizer a violet color, but allows all the pearl effect to shine through.

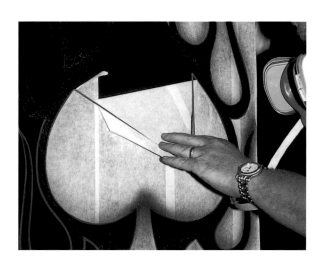

STEP 9

Although it's pretty difficult to see until it's cleared, the violet marblizer snaps against the black background after it's unmasked. Just remember, marblizer is pretty weak. You can easily remove it with precleaner or lift it with tape. So when unmasking, be sure to remove the tape away from the painted surface so that the tape will not lift any edges.

STEP 10

Mix up some lime green by combining lemon yellow and green striping urethane, and then begin striping the marblized design. For graphics and curving designs, the sword striper is ideal. The brush shown above is a size #00.

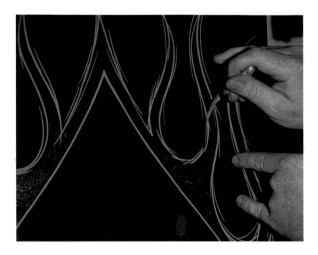

STEP 11

For the outside of the design, keep the same color, but switch to the infamous slash striping. Using this random slash pattern, the outline of the flame graphic is completed.

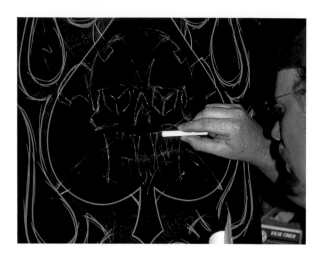

STEP 12

Using a piece of classroom chalk, sketch out the basic design that follows with the pinstriping. This sketch helps establish balance and keeps the design centered. Graphite or waxed-based pencils have a tendency to leave marks behind, especially when clear coating.

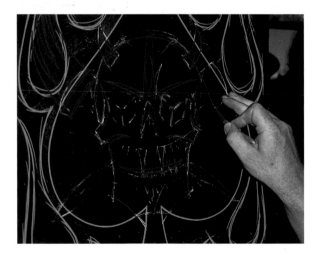

STEP 13

After cleaning the brush and switching to red striping urethane, begin striping the centerpiece design. Right-handers start on the left side of the design; left-handers start on the right side. This prevents your hand from resting in wet paint or blocking your line of sight.

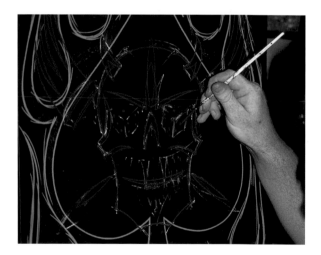

STEP 14

For the dots on the dice, switch from a sword striper to a lettering quill. This allows you to brush in small details that would be difficult to do with a striping brush. This brush would have worked for the entire center design, but the tapered end lines of the striper give a nicer look.

STEP 15

Switching back to the sword striper, use white urethane to punch out the skull design and render the teeth. It is very important to completely clean the brush when switching colors, especially with red. One molecule of red can turn a gallon of white to pink.

STEP 16

Switch back to the liner brush to touch up any ends and to add a few finishing touches to the white, like the trademark number 13 on the tooth.

STEP 17

Using the same lemon yellow that was mixed to make the lime green earlier, lay in the last color of the design. The yellow defines the crossed brushes in the background, as well as the skull's goatee and flame hairdo. A few more colors could be added, but choosing fewer colors keeps the pinstriping clean and simple.

STEP 18

Don't forget the signature. Not signing your artwork is a cardinal sin in pinstriping, especially if you want to get credit for it later on.

Well, that's it. The only thing left is to clear coat with urethane clear.

The best thing about custom painting is the individuality of it. Custom, by definition, has always gone against the grain, thumbing its nose at convention and the established way of doing things. Custom painting is the art of the individual, and the painter must be an individual as well. This is true even if that individual is an airbrusher who just happened to get his hands on a pinstripe brush one day.

SCREAMING eagle

BY JACK "THE ITALIAN" GIACHINO

Jack "The Italian" Giachino has been doing custom paint work and teaching art for more than 30 years. Raised on Von Dutch, Dean Jeffries, and Larry Watson techniques, Giachino says he was "bit by the custom bug" at a very young age. Today he enjoys working with the mixed bag of multimedia techniques and styles he's picked up over the years. His shop specializes in airbrush art, pinstriping, lettering, and design work.

Here are his steps in tackling a screaming eagle paint job:

MATERIALS & EQUIPMENT

White, yellow, red mixing colors
Urethane striping paint
#2 script brush
#00 striping brush
Double-action internal mix airbrush
Transparent masking film (low-tack)
X-Acto knife
White graphite pencil
Clear coat
2,000-grit wet/dry sandpaper
Reducer

STEP 1

Sketch the flame layout and the eagle image to lay a strong foundation for the design.

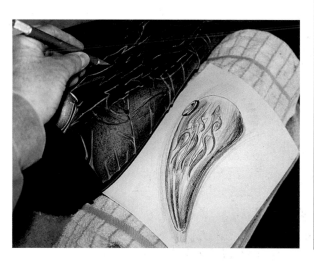

STEP 2

Next, apply the transparent masking film, a low-tack masking material, to both sides of the gas tank. Draw the flame and rip the design directly onto the film with a white graphite pencil. Then use the X-acto knife to carefully cut the design.

STEP 3

Care must be taken not to cut too deeply. Cuts that go well into the painted surface can cause serious problems down the road. Remove the ripped areas around the flames. This is the first part to be airbrushed.

STEP 4

Tape a hand-cut stencil of the eagle's head and claw rips to the top of the tank. Using a combination of white, yellow, and red oxide, airbrush random streaks from the top of the tank, angling forward to the sides. This color combination depicts the wrap of the eagle's wings.

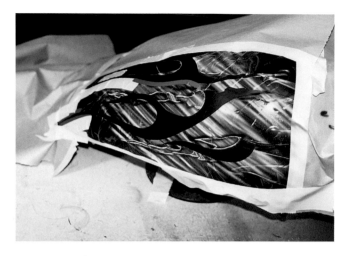

STEP 5

Apply the rip in a random striated pattern and replace
the transparent masking film in these areas. The next
step is to remove the masking film from both sides of
the tank to reveal the flame pattern.

STEP 6

Airbrush the yellow flame base color first, then follow
this with a red undershadow and a white highlight. Sit
the tank on a revolving pottery stand to allow you to
work from one side to the other with ease.

STEP 7

After the masking film is removed from both sides of the
tank, the design starts to take shape. The paints used
so far have all been mixing colors (toners) thinned to
the proper consistency for airbrushing (approximately
twice the recommended spray gun reduction).

STEP 8

Using a photocopy machine, make three copies of the
original eagle design on card stock. This allows
different parts to be cut out for different colors. More
important, it allows for perfect registration of all the
elements, since all three are exact copies.

STEP 9

Mask the stencils to define the sharp edges in the design. Next, freehand the soft-edge areas with a double-action internal mix airbrush.

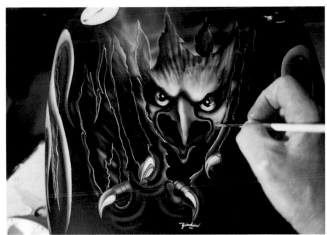

STEP 10

With the bulk of the airbrushing complete, it's time for the finishing touches. Use a #2 script brush to add details and highlights. Note the micro-signature.

STEP 11

The flames wouldn't be complete without pinstriping. A #00 brush and urethane striping paint ensure that this project can be clear-coated without any fear of the pinstriping lifting.

STEP 12

The finished pinstriping adds a framing effect to the flames. Just as the frame completes a picture, the pinstriping completes the flames. After this step, clear coat the tank, color-sand it with 2,000-grit wet/dry sandpaper, buff it, and reassemble it.

the FLAMING helmet

BY CRAIG FRASER

One of the fastest-growing fields in customizing is the aftermarket helmet-painting industry. Ranging from motorcycles and Indy cars to sports like hockey and cycling, the market for individualized helmets has doubled in the past few years. If you have a little motivation and a well-ventilated garage, you can make a sizable dent in this industry.

Helmet costs range from $100 to over $1,000 for a custom-made helmet, and the cost of customizing is fairly high too. Although many helmet owners are happy with their factory sticker kits, nothing is quite as expressive as a custom-painted helmet. In all the motorsports arenas, the rider is considered practically naked if he's not sporting a full-blown custom-painted helmet. This market has grown so large that many automotive painters and airbrush artists have begun specializing solely in spraying helmets.

In this project, we used a rather simple helmet, so that the process was not lost in all the airbrush tricks.

This particular helmet was done for Steve Stillwell, editor of *Hot Bike* magazine. Steve wanted something unique on his brain bucket. He wanted it to be a classic design but also wanted it to have some airbrushing. The helmet also had to match the kandy color of his bike and the flames. Nothing like a little challenge.

The helmet used is known in the industry as a half-helmet or beanie. Be aware that beanies aren't legal in all states.

Although Steve's helmet was used, even brand-new helmets should be prepped, which involves removing stickers on or under the gel coat clear. For durability and quality of finish, we used only urethane-based products.

Although the techniques covered in this chapter were applied to a little peanut helmet, remember that 90 percent of all helmets are made in the same manner, with gel coat skins. These same techniques also apply to hockey helmets, baseball helmets, NASCAR helmets, skiing helmets, and even bicycle helmets.

STEP 1

Disassemble the helmet, mask off the underside, and sand the black gel-coated surface with 220-grit sandpaper. It's necessary to sand and reseal the gel coat, due to mold-release waxes in it that can reactivate later, causing lifting or bubbling of the clear if not sealed properly.

STEP 2

After sanding the entire surface, spray it with a catalyzed polyester sealer. This sealer/primer locks in the mold-release waxes and gives a good, sandable foundation for the upcoming paint. Any nicks or scratches are taken care of at this stage with a catalyzed polyester filler.

STEP 3

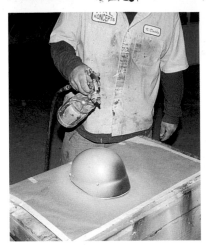

After giving the primer a few hours to fully dry, spray on a combination of HoK Orion Silver Basecoat and HoK Solar Gold. This base gives the Kandy Apple a deep metallic look.

STEP 4

Notice the slight gold shimmer of the metallic. The gold is necessary in the painting of a true Kandy Apple paint job. It decreases the brightness of the red kandy and gives it a richer glow than if it was solely shot with a silver base.

STEP 5

Starting with a tack coat first, dust the plate and helmet with HoK UK-11 catalyzed Kandy Red. The tack coat provides an important tooth for the subsequent wet coats to adhere to. Without the tack coat, it's common for any additional coats to run, especially on curved surfaces such as this helmet.

STEP 6

After applying three additional wet coats of kandy, the true color of the helmet begins to show through. It's important not to give the helmet too many coats of kandy: besides the obvious running and sagging problem, the kandy will also continue to darken. A true kandy will darken until it appears black. This may be desirable for some effects, but not if you're trying to match a lighter shade of kandy already on the bike.

STEP 7

Apply a protective coat of clear after the previous color coat. Then let the helmet set for 24 hours before sanding in preparation for the airbrush work. Using 600-grit wet/dry sandpaper, knock down the shine to provide a good surface to work on. The design is then lightly sketched using pure white chalk. It wipes off easily and leaves no residue to interfere with the clear coat.

STEP 8

Continue the sketching process using an airbrush. The brains and breaks in the helmet are retraced and detailed over the chalk sketch. (Nitride rubber gloves are great for artists who are sensitive to reducers.) Of course, the aluminum skull support for the helmet is an absolute necessity.

STEP 9

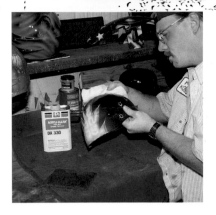

After finishing the white, wipe the entire surface with a damp rag and precleaner. This removes any of the excess chalk as well as overspray. Do this wipe-down process after every color change, making a clean surface for every step and preventing buildup of dry areas caused by overspray.

STEP 10

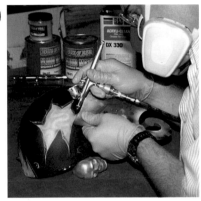

Donning Superman gloves, come back with some HoK SG-101 Lemon Yellow Basecoat. A freehand shield allows you to control the overspray and give the area a sharp, soft edge without the buildup a taped edge would give—not to mention that the freehand shield is a heck of a lot faster and leaves no tape residue.

STEP 11

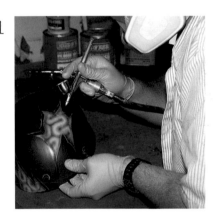

Next, build up the detail using a mixture of Tangerine, Root Beer, and Pagan Gold Kandy Koncentrates mixed with intercoat clear. The result is a transparent red oxide that works nicely in sculpting the brains.

STEP 12

The darkest areas of the details were done with a mixture of transparent Violette and Cobalt Blue Kandy Koncentrate and intercoat clear. This creates a deep purple that appears as red/brown when layered over the red oxide and yellow. Continuous layering gives the illusion of black in the detail without killing any of the colors.

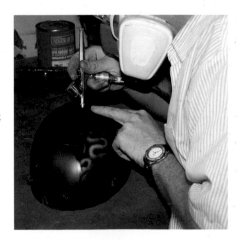

STEP 13

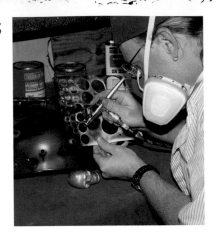

To create the realistic bullet holes in the sides, use an architectural circle template. The purple kandy mixture is used with a few drops of black added to it. The black makes the bullet holes stand out from the details in the brains and gives them more depth.

STEP 14

Last but not least, the highlights and rising smoke from the holes are airbrushed in white. To get the extra-fine detail in the broken-edged highlights and thin wisps, use the Iwata Micron-C airbrush. The white is even further reduced, to prevent spitting and clogging at this detail range.

STEP 15

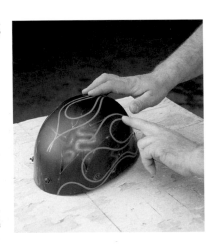

With the airbrushing done, the helmet is given a light coat of clear to protect it from the masking. Non-catalyzed intercoat clear is used because it has a drying window of only one hour. The surface is then scuffed to prepare for the flame layout. The flames are laid out using 1/8-inch blue fine line tape. Fineline tape is perfect for helmets, since it can turn a radius without bunching and is repositionable.

STEP 16

After the blue fine line tape is applied, mask up to the edge with 3/4-inch masking tape, to cover the surrounding area of the shell. With the previous batch of SG-101 Lemon Yellow Basecoat, paint the flames with the Eclipse airbrush. The Eclipse not only has a wider spray pattern, but the bottle allows you to spray longer without refills.

STEP 17

Mixing up more of the red oxide concoction, spray a light orange fade on the tips of the flames. A little Lavender Dry Pearl added to the red oxide kandy gives a deep red color when layered over the yellow.

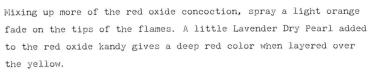

STEP 18

After the tape is removed and the surface is wiped down with precleaner again (tape residue!), use a freehand shield to help lay in the drop shadows under the flames. The drop shadow is sprayed using a transparent over-reduced mixture of Basecoat Black.

STEP 19

Then switch to a sword striper brush. With a little HoK Lite Blue urethane striping paint, carefully pull a line around the flames. Practicing striping on an old helmet is an excellent way to build up brush control and mastery.

STEP 20

The helmet is then taken into the booth and clear coated. The painter uses his trusty Iwata LPH-95 to lay down a tack coat and three good wet coats of HoK UFC-35 Komply Klear. While a helmet normally needs one final clearing session, this one may need to be sanded and cleared again to eliminate the pinstripe edge. Clear coated, polished, and reassembled, this helmet is ready to ship back to Stillwell in time for the "Loveride."

PART 3

furling CHECKERS

BY CRAIG FRASER

One of the most recognizable designs in automotive graphics, aside from the flame, is the checkerboard pattern. Seen throughout the racing industry, it is the international symbol for victory. Used throughout the custom paint industry for years, it continues to be a hard-hitting symbol, even in today's newest hybrid styles. But you can even tweak classic symbols a bit to give them a new look.

This design takes the classic international symbol of victory and gives it a little twist. But the result is a new style that looks hot on any surface and makes a cool demo. It's a bit labor intensive, so don't commit yourself at first to a large area when painting this design—start with something small like a helmet.

MATERIALS & EQUIPMENT
Transfer tape
Transparent masking film
Felt-tip marker
X-acto knife
Black, lemon yellow, white base coat
Violet, cobalt blue, tangerine candy
Blue, lavender dry pearl
Clear coat
Reducer
Metallic silver striping urethane
#1 lettering quill
Top-feed airbrush
Touch-up gun
Plastic vinyl squeegee or spreader
Freehand shield
Precleaner

STEP 1

Using the top-feed gun, spray the prepped metal sign blank with lemon yellow. Since a checkerboard design incorporates both extremes of light and dark (black and white), a bright color such as yellow helps to create contrast with the design.

STEP 2

After the yellow dries, apply the transfer tape. By applying it right off the roll, you can eliminate the wrinkling and bubbling that can occur by precutting the paper into sheets. As you've seen in other demos, you can eliminate these bubbles using a simple plastic vinyl squeegee. If you don't have a vinyl squeegee, you can always use a spreader.

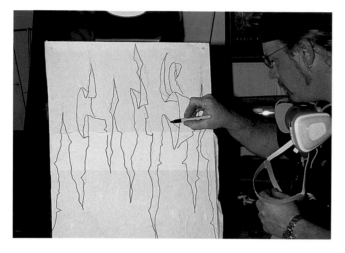

STEP 3

Using the felt-tip marker, lay out the furls and uneven edges of the flag. Even though you'll want the rips and shreds to look completely random, there's still a semblance of order and balance to the design. This is important when laying out graphics on a vehicle. While a little contrast with the design of the vehicle is good, you still need to preserve the lines of the car.

STEP 4

With the X-acto knife, cut out the design and peel back the paper. Since this entire design must be cut out with a blade (laying out a design like this can be a quick road to insanity), it's important to remember to use a sharp blade. A dull blade will quickly score your paint and may even cause lifting in your graphics.

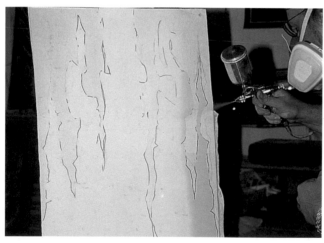

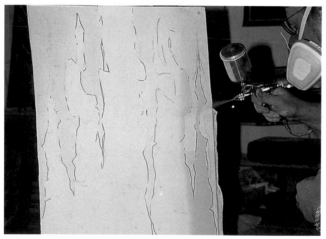

STEP 5

Going back to the smaller touch-up gun, spray down the exposed area with white base coat. Though you would normally reduce the base coat in a 1:1 ratio for airbrushing, with the larger spray gun, a ratio of 2:1 (2 parts paint:1 part reducer) provides better coverage.

STEP 6

After giving the white coat time to dry, place another sheet of transfer tape over the design on which to lay out the checkers. Due to its high transparency compared to masking tape, the underlying design will be visible and this will help in the layout.

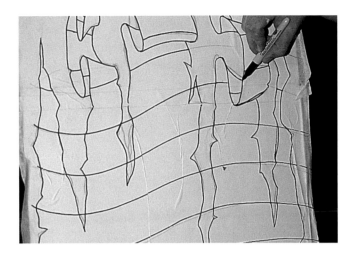

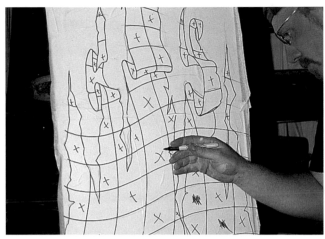

STEP 7

Using the felt-tip marker, begin laying out the checkerboard design. To make the furl effect more realistic, give the checkerboard pattern a slight curve. The rule of thumb here is that no matter what direction and shape you give the pattern, you must keep the checked boxes consistent in size.

STEP 8

Give the vertical grid a slight curve to mimic the horizontal lines. Notice how even though the shapes of the checks vary, the sizes remain similar. A slight variation can give a 3-D effect, but too much will just make the layout look sloppy. Mark the checked boxes to be removed with an "X." This may sound simplistic, but it's easy to make a cutting mistake at this stage.

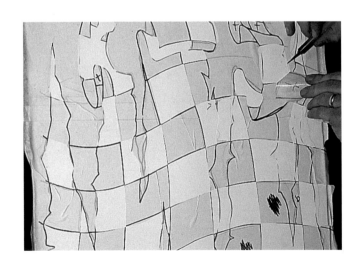

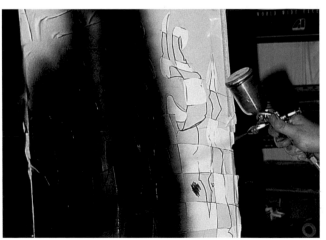

STEP 9

Cut one more time with the X-acto knife. (This is definitely a demo where, if you weren't good with a blade before this graphic, you'll be an expert by the time you're done.) If this were a straight checkerboard, you would layer 1-inch tape to form the grid, a faster method that lessens the amount of cutting.

STEP 10

Cleaning the white out of the mini-gun, spray the masked checks with black base coat. A touch-up gun is perfect for small graphics such as this, since it's easy to clean, doesn't spray too much material, and the tape edge doesn't get too coated.

STEP 11

At this point it can get confusing. When there is a double-masking system involved, it's important to make sure you don't pull the wrong piece of tape. Of course, you can always re-mask any mistake with a bit of scrap tape. (Don't beat yourself up over it.)

STEP 12

Mix a combination of violet and cobalt blue kandy and spray in some streaks and shadows to give the flag an added furled effect. A touch of blue dry pearl added to the mix gives the flag a nice glow too. Little touches like this keep your graphics looking fresh and different.

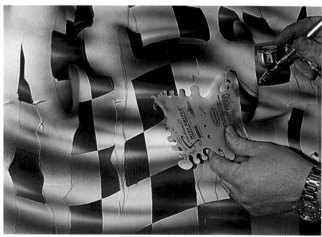

STEP 13

To create tight furls and darker shadows, add a little black to the violet mix in the top-feed airbrush, and pick up the freehand shield to help keep the lines sharp, but soft. (Be careful with the black at this stage; too much will muddy up the checker design, and you'll lose the sharp effect you created with your masking.)

STEP 14

When airbrushing, white is even more dangerous than black where overspray is concerned. While white improves the flag's three dimensionality 100 percent, it can also wipe out the design if you use it too much. Remember the rule of all design: Less is more.

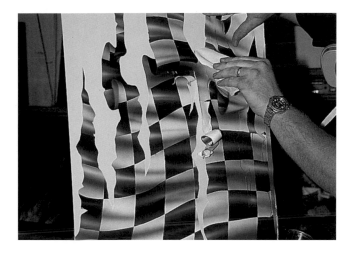

STEP 15

Once the airbrushing is done in the flag design, unmask the shreds and wipe down the entire surface with precleaner. It's important to get all the residue removed. Any glue, overspray, or dirt will not only show up when cleared, but also be amplified.

STEP 16

As a transition color between the checkered flag and the yellow background, airbrush in a mixture of tangerine kandy and clear coat. A little lavender pearl in the mix adds to the background glow and ties in with the violet of the checkers.

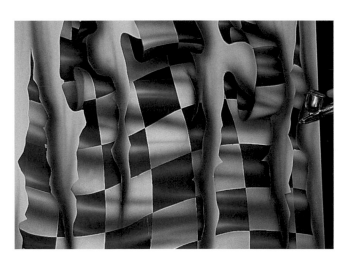

STEP 17

Add a touch of black base coat to the tangerine and bring in the drop shadows of the design to give the shreds one more added illusion of furling and floating above the yellow background. Of all the techniques that are important to master in automotive airbrushing, drop shadows are in the top three. Not because it's the most important effect, but because it's difficult to keep a gradated fade clean. An airbrusher's ability is often judged on this simple technique. No freehand stencil can help you with this.

STEP 18

Like many of the effects in this book, the final step before clearing is pinstriping. Using metallic silver urethane striping enamel, lay on the stripe with a #1 lettering quill. On tight corners and curves, the fastest and cleanest brushes are often the short-haired quills and not the sword stripers.

diamond
PLATING

BY CRAIG FRASER

Custom painters not only have to deliver quality at a competitive price, but they also have to keep up with the newest styles and hip effects. To stay in the business, painters must have a pulse on the latest trend, or take the initiative to lead the pack by experimenting and creating their own effects. But constant experimentation can take a toll on a painter's work. One shortcut to innovation is to take what is common practice in another industry and adopt it.

A good example of this is seen in the vinyl graphics field. The technology that sign makers have used for years has now found its way into the automotive industry in the form of predesigned vinyl graphics. But the great thing about this industry is that no matter how innovative an idea may appear, there are always ways to improve upon it. For example, vinyl will never replace graphics, no matter how much a painter airbrushes on it. Most people will always view them as stickers. The trick is to use vinyl technology to improve the one aspect of the industry that has shown little development in the last 20 years: masking. Bob Bond pioneered this concept with his Splash mask system, and he and many others contributed to CD-ROM graphics packages such as Vector Art's systems.

In this project, you'll see how to combine computer design programs, vinyl cutters, and airbrushing into the diamond plate effect—once extremely time-consuming and a major pain.

Of all the automotive effects, this is one of the few that was borrowed from the illustration field. The concept was first debuted at SEMA on a 1996 Ford Prototype F-150.

The effect was created using a freehand shield and many hours of time. But this newly modified demo explains how you can use the computer to take the drudgery out of positioning, layout, and cutting your design without using a soggy, dog-eared stencil and masking tape.

MATERIALS & EQUIPMENT

Vinyl design and cutting program
Cutter/plotter
Personal computer
Masking tape
Scouring pad
Precleaner
X-acto knife
Plastic vinyl squeegee
Transfer tape
Circle template
Silver, black, white base coat
Tangerine, root beer candy
Clear coat
Reducer
Freehand shield
Top-feed airbrush
Touch-up gun

STEP 1

Using the design program on your computer, work up a diamond plate design that closely resembles the plate of a boat trailer. The design should include a small border around each piece that the plotter cuts out. This border mask is used to show the beveled edge created when the diamond plate is punched out during fabrication (another big thanks to Joe Calabrese of Air Graphix Inc.)

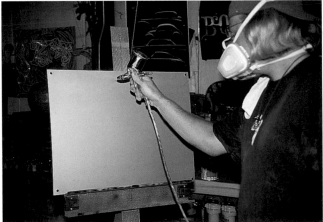

STEP 2

Using the touch-up gun, spray an even coat of silver base coat. This gives the diamond plate a good metallic base to heighten the realism of the finish. (Remember to wear a respirator. Anytime you airbrush or paint urethanes, wear a good dual-cartridge respirator rated for organic vapors, and work in an area that is well ventilated. Because of some of the caustic pigments in many of the "non-toxic" water-based paints, it's a good idea to wear a mask when you're using them, too. Better safe than sorry.)

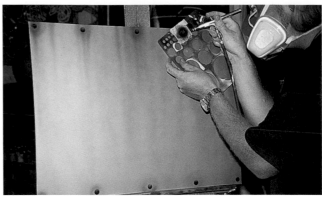

STEP 3

Switching to the top-feed airbrush, create water-stain marks, streaking, and distress marks in the metal surface using over-reduced black base coat mixed with a little silver. Whenever you work over a metallic surface like silver, it's a good idea to add a little of the original silver into any of your opaque pigments. This gives the paint a similar incidence of refraction with the light source. In short, without the silver, any opaque paint will appear to float above the metal surface.

STEP 4

Using a masked-off architectural circle template, lay in some rivets along the top and bottom. This not only helps the metal panel effect, but also hides any drill holes that were already in the panel. Using the same black/silver mixture, make sure it is overly reduced to prevent any of the airbrushing from standing out too much. After all, it is the background treatment.

STEP 5

To bring a little color into the piece, create some rust deterioration. This is accomplished using a mixture of tangerine and root beer kandy. Since these are transparent kandies, there's no need to add the silver for it to blend in with the piece. The silver underneath will come through due to the transparency factor. This color can also be achieved using red oxide.

STEP 6

With the underlying metal treatment done, cut off a section of the pre-cut diamond plate mask. Borrowing an old signmaker's trick, lay the sheet on the board using the "butterfly" technique. This is where you first center the design, then tape the middle, and peel each side independently before sticking it to the surface. Not only is this technique a major time saver in aligning a piece, but it helps to prevent a lot of nasty bubbles that have a tendency to show up at inopportune moments.

STEP 7

Using a plastic vinyl squeegee, burnish the vinyl into the surface before unmasking the transfer tape and get rid of any rogue bubbles. Flatten them to prevent any paint bleeding.

STEP 8

With the surface smooth and all the bubbles sent to bubble hell, carefully remove the transfer tape. The "carefully" is important in this step; if you get too gung-ho, you can accidentally remove half of your vinyl masking as well. For the "sign illiterate," the transfer tape is used to hold the cut vinyl together while pulling off the backing paper and allows you to transfer the design to the surface, then peel it away so you can get to the masked area. (Pretty kewl. What will these sign guys think of next?)

STEP 9

Now the fun part of signage work, the weeding. (The real reason they call it weeding is because it's about as much fun as weeding the lawn.) Using an X-acto knife, lift out all the individual borders that the computer cut around the initial diamond design. These are going to be painted a lighter color, with the surrounding area remaining masked, to give the illusion of an external light source reflecting off of them.

STEP 10

Notice the top and bottom of the board is masked off to prevent any overspray. This is important, especially when using silver. (That stuff loves to float around and stick on important surfaces, and not show up until after it's cleared.) Using the same top-feed airbrush, spray a mixture of silver and white on the unmasked beveled area.

STEP 11

After giving the paint about 15 minutes to set, begin pulling away the mask. Remove the masking as soon as it's painted on to prevent the urethane from hardening the vinyl, which can cause a problem with removal.

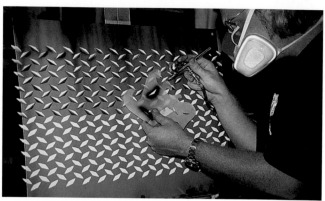

STEP 12

Here's a good example of what can happen when you're too busy running back and forth with your camera and airbrush and you forget a step. The bottom edge of the bevel wasn't hit with the black/silver mixture for the underlying, shadowed side of the diamond before the masking was taken off. Don't worry, there's no need to re-mask everything. Cut a small triangle shape out of the freehand shield that matches the bottom edge of the diamond, then use the tried-and-true method of freehand masking and individually spray each diamond.

STEP 13

To give the diamonds an added sense of depth, freehand in a gradated drop shadow under each one. For the drop shadow, use a transparent black solution with no silver since you want the shadow to have no opacity, just merely darken the existing area. The center diamond faces are still masked, so you don't have to worry about overspray on the top areas from the shadowing. No matter what masking system you use, you should always add freehand touches. This not only softens the edges, but adds a personalized touch to your work and prevents your finished piece from looking like an airbrushed sticker.

STEP 14

With the freehand airbrush sculpting done, remove the remainder of the masking from the diamond centers. After all the unmasking is completed, wipe the entire surface with a cloth dampened with water and precleaner. This will remove any adhesive residues and overspray that may have stuck to the surface. Don't make it a point to scrub the surface. You don't want to rub off your airbrushed shading.

STEP 15

Going back with a transparent mixture of black and root beer toner, continue some of the streaks down the surface. Again, this freehanding blends in the hard masked areas and, since the urethane toners are transparent, the detailed edges will show through, adding to the realism and three-dimensionality of the design. Plus, it fools all the masking gurus and masking film freaks into thinking you did multiple layers of masking to get all the varied colors and shades. Remember, keep it easy. In the immortal words of Mies Vanderow: "Less is more." Really, how complicated can diamond plate be?

STEP 16

Using the circle template one final time, hit a small highlight on the top round of every rivet with the airbrush and silver/white mixture used earlier, just a little more over-reduced. Be careful when making these final touches. The last thing you want to do is kill your piece with too many highlights or white highlight overspray. Leave the individual diamonds alone.

STEP 17

Well, there you have it: a nice example of how to render a realistic effect using combined media. Apply a coat of clear and you've got a great demo panel to hang on your wall or take to shows. Playing with sign blanks gives you a good stockpile of examples and provides a good practice surface without having to experiment on the 350-pound Harley owner's pride and joy.

This vinyl system of masking opens new doors of painting previously ignored because of the tedium or impossibility of masking. However, it can also be a trap. Freehand techniques are just as important, if not more so, when working with masking to protect against the sticker look. Freehand shields and moveable masks are still important tools for touchups.

Vinyl masking systems, CD-ROM graphic files, and computer-generated designs are not the answer to every painter's masking dilemma. But they are useful tools that elevate the quality of a custom paint job to another level. It's important to note that using vinyl doesn't make you an automotive painter, just as using a computer design program doesn't make you an artist—it's just an important addition to your arsenal of time-saving tricks.

pic—STRIPING

BY MIKE LAVALLEE

Pinstriping and murals come in a huge variety of styles, from the traditional striping of the 1950s to the scroll and high-tech artwork of today. "Pic-striping," which merges pictures and stripes, is another one of those styles. The technique for hand-painted pictorial work is a dry-brush method, where you build up colors by loosely applying one color over the next with very little thinner used in the paint. Of course, this is not the only way to paint, but give pic-striping a try. It's a lot of fun, and you'll open a whole new world for yourself.

Remember this phrase: dark to light, loose to tight. Always work from the darkest colors to the lightest. Keep things super loose and gradually get tighter and brighter with the details and colors until you reach your goal. You may find this method confusing at first, but when you see your artwork develop, you'll understand why this works so well. Painting this way allows you to work faster and produce pictures with more life.

The first thing to do is find excellent reference material. Nothing can replace a great photo of your subject. This will help you get started and serve as your guide to detail and color. Also, when choosing a picture, select one that works well with the shape of the panel you'll paint on. For instance, an eagle head profile works better on the side of a motorcycle tank than it would, say, on the top of the tank.

Second, always clean the surface of whatever you're working on with a good wax and grease remover. Then wipe the surface with window cleaner to remove any residue from the wax and grease remover. After cleaning, give the surface the old finger squeak test to ensure that it's completely free of wax.

MATERIALS & EQUIPMENT
1/2-inch flat pictorial brush
#4050 script brush
White graphite paper
Orange, purple, black, white, yellow, blue,
    lemon yellow, teal enamels
Wax and grease remover
Window cleaner

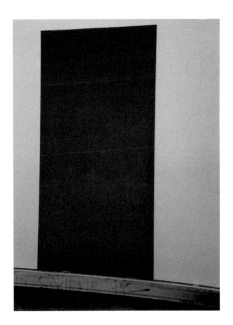
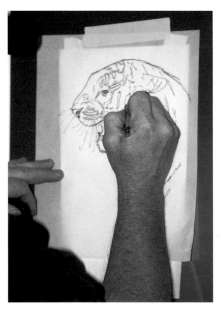

STEP 1

Tape the sketch of the picture (in this demo a picture of a tiger was used) to the panel and place the white graphite paper under the sketch. (Make sure the chalky side is down before you start to trace your picture. Only the chalky side will leave a traced image for you to follow.) Trace over the major shapes of the tiger. You don't have to trace all the little details—just go over the outer body shape, eye, nose, mouth, white patches, and black stripes. Now you can see the tiger transferred on the panel.

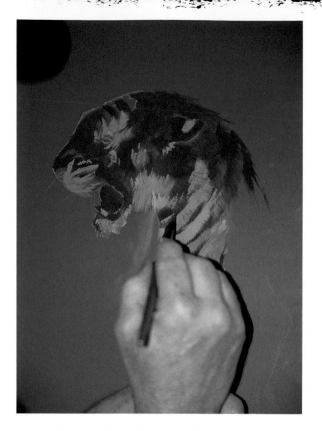

STEP 2

Start painting with very little thinner. You want your
paint to drag slightly and break up when you apply it.
This is called a dry-brush effect. By doing this, you
allow each color to be seen though the next so that each
layer works together to create a whole piece. Use the
1/2-inch flat brush for the bulk of this pictorial. When
you load the brush, palette off about 50 percent of the
paint to avoid flooding the color.

STEP 3

Next, mix a bit of white, black, and purple to get the dark
color for the base of all the white. Paint this the same
way you did the first color, letting the paint break apart
as you go along. Some of the original panel color should
still be visible through the paint at this point. Slightly
overlap the purple and white paint over the first color.

Start with orange mixed about 50-50 with purple to get
a brownish purple color. If the paint becomes too
sticky, dip slightly into a thinner cup. Dry-brush the
dark color where the orange of the tiger is. Paint in the
direction of the hair, constantly referring to the original
photo for the correct look. Your strokes should be
shorter where the hair is shorter and longer where it is
longer. Don't be too concerned with making this first
4.3-perfect. Remember, loose to tight! Lay in some
loose detail to show the nose outline and the teeth.

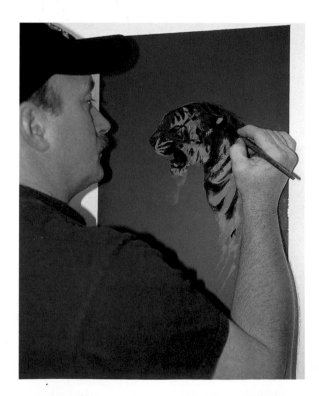

STEP 4

Move on to roughing in the black stripes and dark colors in
the mouth area. For this step, mix purple and orange with a
touch of black to make a brownish color. This is the only step
where you don't go dark to light. Roughly paint in the brown
color with the same "hair" strokes in all the areas. Trace out
the tiger's stripes and then, more solidly, in the mouth area.
To soften the stripes and make them look more realistic, use
brown first, instead of going right to black. Otherwise, the
stripes would just be stark black. When you do add black,
blend the color only within the brown you already painted,
leaving some of that brown color showing around the edges.

STEP 5

Now you'll bring the cat to life! Take straight orange and palette some into your brush. Remember to take most of it out by paletting on a magazine page so only a medium amount of paint remains on the hairs. Start the whole process over by brushing the hair over the darker color you painted first. Let the first color show through a bit to add depth to the hair. You can lighten this color some more by adding a touch of white or yellow in smaller amounts where you see brighter highlights in your original reference photo. Add some of the orange color to the eye and highlight it with the lighter yellow-orange color.

STEP 6

Do the same thing to the areas that you'll paint white, repeating the same process you used for the orange, only this time use straight white. While you have the white out, mix up a little pinkish brown and paint the nose and tongue. Then lighten up that color and highlight these areas.

STEP 7

It's time to use the black paint. As mentioned earlier, when you paint in the black on the stripes, paint only the centers with the "hair" strokes and leave a bit of the original color showing around the edges. It's like a "glow line," if you will. Next, move on to the mouth. At this point, switch to the script brush to do some of the smaller line details, such as outlining the teeth and detailing around the eye and nose.

STEP 8

It's time to finesse the cat's coat with all the little details in the white fur. To do this, look for spots that need to be punched up. Add some flare to the fur around the cheek area, and then go in and add some small white highlights to the nose and eye.

STEP 9

The cat is almost complete. You just have to jazz up this picture with some color. Start by using blue and dry-brushing some graphic shreds. Load the brush as before, taking most of the paint off. Then, using the corner of the 1/2-inch flat pictorial brush, start at the top of the tiger's head and paint small ragged strokes in a broken fashion. The strokes get larger the farther away from the head you work, in the same way that the hairs are smaller at the front of the head, growing gradually longer as they go back. Swing this pattern across and in front of the picture. Add touches of blue to the black fur on the ears and the fleshy part of the mouth. Add little tiny specks of this color here and there to add "color tension" to the piece.

STEP 10

The next step is to put some action lines around the cat with some scroll-type pinstriping. Using purple and the script brush, paint some sweeping loops around the tiger's head and neck. The lines should be thin to start, but as you loop around, gradually press harder on the brush to achieve the thicker part of the stroke and then lighten up near the end of the stripe.

This part takes practice to develop the correct speed and movement. Use the hand-over-hand method to hold the brush. Use both hands at the same time—they move as one. Use your non-dominant hand mainly as a brace on which to support and roll your dominant hand, and use the dominant hand to maneuver the brush through the loops and sweeps of the strokes. The non-dominant hand should almost never touch the surface while you paint. The only time it makes contact with the surface is when you start the stroke or when you need to brace your dominant hand while you're painting the little details.

Loop a stroke around the tiger's head to frame it. That loop makes a nice touch.

Well, there you have it—a complete pic-striped design. With some practice, you'll be creating all kinds of combinations and creations! This is a fun way to add some zip to a boring pictorial. Don't be afraid to experiment with different looks and color combinations. After all, it's just paint!

STEP 11

Next, mix a yellow-orange color to outline the thicker strokes of the purple pinstripes. With the same yellow-orange, build on what you've already painted with stripes similar to the purple stripes you painted first, but this time don't outline them.

STEP 12

You're just about done with the pinstriping. The next and final step to give the tiger his whiskers. Wait until the end to do this because then the whiskers will go over the pinstriping. It would be almost impossible to do it the other way around. Take orange and a touch of purple and paint in the whiskers. Then, as before, lighten up the mixture and highlight the whiskers.

the art of the
PINSTRIPE

BY CRAIG FRASER

The art of the pinstripe is one of the oldest techniques in the custom-painting industry. Practiced by many but mastered by few, pinstriping is an art form that combines precision skill with design simplicity, whether you're looking at a brilliant panel jam from Bob Bond or a two-color masterpiece from Von Franco.

The purest art form in the customizing industry, pinstriping straddles the fence between practical application and art. It is often the last thing a painter adds to a vehicle, but far from being just an afterthought, quality pinstriping can elevate a vehicle to show-winning status.

Pinstriping is the old-world art form of the hot rod industry and the true heart of the custom culture. Although airbrushing has become very mainstream, pinstriping has remained largely an underground art form. Many of the tricks and techniques of the trade are relatively unknown to those outside the industry. As part of a thriving subculture, pinstripers even have their own organization, the Pinheads. Stripers are an integral part of all custom painting, but they stand apart from most customizers and painters. While all stripers can paint, few painters can stripe. Yet even with all the panel jams, Pinhead events, custom-culture art shows, and Ed Roth's yearly Rat Fink Reunions, few books document these artists and their work.

Not surprisingly, the main players in the pinstriping industry are a unique breed. These stripers are accomplished practitioners in an industry that demands best-quality work at top speed. Their jobs call for stunningly intricate—yet surprisingly minimalist—line work. While many regard Roth and Kenneth "Von Dutch" Howard as the pioneers of pinstriping, they were actually the pioneers of the "custom" striping era. Pinstriping was around centuries before legendary custom artist "The Baron" had even striped his first Studebaker. Rooted in early heraldry and crest design, pinstriping dates back to a time when cars didn't even exist. The first striping jobs decorated royal carriages and chariots. The artists of striping, whether they're part of the new crowd or the old school, are tied together by a common thread: the brush and the art of the line.

This chapter is dedicated to the art and artists of the pinstriping world. In looking at the individual pinstripers' tricks and techniques, you also see their contribution to the industry and the personal interpretation of the art form itself. Many of the contributing artists in this book have also given a little history about themselves and their experience in the industry. This collection of step-by-step articles is the first of its kind, showing the signature tricks and techniques of the top pinstripers in the industry today. More than just a technical manual, this chapter is a historical documentation of the artist and his art. It is a living tribute to the quintessential custom-culture art form and the individual legends who have made it so.

Paint to live, live to paint.

CHOOSING AND USING YOUR BRUSH

Pinstriping brushes come in many sizes—the bigger the number, the thicker the brush and wider the line. If you're new to pinstriping, start with a #1 or #2 brush. The bigger brush holds more paint, and many beginners have a tendency not to put enough paint on the brush. In reality, you must concentrate on putting paint on your surface, not on your brush. The paint on your brush, however, is very important. It can't be too thin or too thick. It should have just a little drag for the brush to work properly. That means you have to "palette" constantly. Paletting is the single most important aspect of pinstriping. (Basically, paletting means working the brush back and forth on a surface, while alternately dipping it in the paint. This loads the paint into the brush, allowing the brush to pull long even lines.) Not everyone holds the brush the same way—go with whatever feels comfortable for you. But everyone has to "load up" the brush on the palette. You can't paint if your brush doesn't have any paint on it. Practice and palette.

the FRESNO stripe

BY RON BEAM

Based in Bakersfield, California, Ron Beam and his brothers have made their mark in custom painting and pinstriping for the past 25 years. "The Beam Brothers" are known for their incredible work on boats, race cars, and bikes, creating some of the hottest paint jobs to come out of California in the 1970s and 1980s. Their masterpieces graced the show circuit back in the days of the R. G. Canning and World of Wheels shows. If you grew up in central or southern California, you had to have a Beam Brothers paint job on your race car or street machine. While the Beam Brothers team no longer exists, the individual brothers are still doing their own thing. In fact, the business has spread within the family. Bob, the airbrusher, has a sign business in Las Vegas, while his son, Jason (Ron's nephew), has resurrected the Beam racing logo under his fast-growing helmet painting company. With many off-road and racing professionals as clients, Jason Beam is successfully following in the family's footsteps.

Today Ron is one of the hardest working pinstripers in central California. During the last decade, he has been balancing his time between custom work and dealership pinstriping, and he's even in demand on the racing circuit. Since Ron is equally good at one-off customizing and lightning-fast production stripe work, he remains one of the most sought-after stripers in the region. At one point, he had so much work from his regular clientele that he put a message on his answering machine stating that he was out of business! Fortunately, that didn't work. People just showed up at the shop and peeked in to see if he could cram in one more striping job.

When it comes to rock-solid straight lines, no one touches Ron. Follow along as he demonstrates some of his trademark pinstriping, including his famous "Fresno Stripe."

MATERIALS & EQUIPMENT
Red, gray, white lettering enamel
Striping brushes
#3 lettering quill
#00 sword striper
Degreaser
Precleaner
1/4-inch green masking tape
Yardstick

STEP 1
Before any striping job, wipe the entire surface down with a good degreaser. This product removes road grime and takes off any wax on the surface that may prevent the paint from sticking. After using the degreaser, remember to wax the surrounding area again after the job is finished and dry.

STEP 2
Using the 1/4-inch green masking tape, lay out the basic graphic "thick" line. This tape works well to guide the paint, and it's also very easy to pull off the tape and reposition it when making long straight lines. While blue fineline vinyl tape may turn corners better, the green stuff leaves behind less adhesive residue.

STEP 3

Give yourself room for a stripe that
is about 3/8 inch wide and mask it
off for painting. For this part,
measure out the line. (But when
you've been striping as long as
Ron has, your eye is as good as
any ruler.)

STEP 4

Mixing up a batch of red, palette
your brush and paint on the nearest
phone book. Keeping the paint in a
cup saves the can from drying out.
You can dip some catalyst and
reducer on the brush to help the
paint dry faster and flow better.

STEP 5

Using a #3 lettering quill, brush in
the main graphic stripe.

STEP 6

The main graphic flares into a wedge-shaped design on the back of the bed. Use the brush to freehand the inside area.

STEP 7

Pull the tape before the paint completely dries. Although you have to be careful when doing this, it's well worth it—the edge will soften on its own if the paint is still pliable.

STEP 8

With all the striping unmasked, clean up any mistakes with a rag and some precleaner. It's best to catch these mistakes early on, before the paint has a chance to dry.

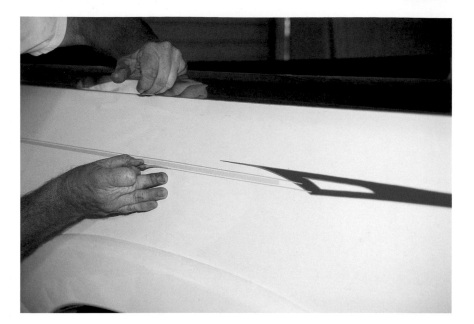

STEP 9

Using the tape as a visual guide,
pull a similar line along the bottom
edge of the tape.

STEP 10

Mixing up a dark gray, begin pulling
the border lines with the #00 sword
striper. Here's the famous Fresno
Stripe—border stripes over a thicker
center line.

STEP 11

After laying another piece of tape
behind the graphic, add a bit of
white to the gray to get a lighter
shade and begin pulling some
parallel lines. Run your finger
along the tape edge to guide your
hand as you stripe.

STEP 12

After pulling the tape, pull a third line between the two. Multiple parallel lines help fill space and emphasize the linear design.

STEP 13

You can add a single-line graphic in the space between the Fresno line and the body trim of the truck. Using the same 1/4-inch tape, lay out the guidelines.

STEP 14

Using the same #00 sword striper, palette the brush with an even lighter version of gray and trace the outline of your guide tape design.

STEP 15

Going back to red, lay in some cool teardrop scallops along the leading edge of the gray single-line graphic.

STEP 16

Use the same red and gray to spice up the top graphic with a little "hoop-de-do."

STEP 17
Use the gray to outline and emphasize the teardrop graphic.

STEP 18
Here's the finished classic Fresno striping job. The simple Fresno line may not be as radical as some of Ron's hot rod paintwork, but it definitely pays the bills, especially when you can crank lines out as fast as Ron can!

pinstriping with a STRIPING wheel

BY DON EDWARDS

Beuglers are ideal for striping, from straight lines to scrolls to outlining flames and graphics. Although traditionalists still consider using this tool to be cheating, if you stripe large scroll patterns (or just don't like refilling your brush while standing on a ladder), give the Beugler a try. You won't learn overnight, but in time you will find it to be a valuable tool in your striping kit.

MATERIALS & EQUIPMENT

Lettering enamel
Sword striper
Craft paper
Pounce wheel and pad
Sandpaper
Degreaser
Striping wheel
Magnetic guide strip
Masking tape
Yardstick
Chalk or pounce bag

STEP 1

Using craft paper, draw a center line and freehand half of a scroll pattern with a pencil. You can create a grid pattern to help with design balance. Working on a soft background (like rubber or soft wood), perforate holes along half the design with a pounce wheel.

STEP 2

Fold the pattern along the center line so the back of the pounced side is now facing you. Lightly sand the paper to open the holes made by the pounce wheel. Take a pounce bag and rub it across the perforated holes. (You can make a pounce bag with powdered charcoal in an old T-shirt or even construction chalk in a sock.) Next, reopen the paper and use the pounce wheel on the other half of the design. You can use the imprint left from the first side as your guide. When this side is finished, sand the whole back. Now you are ready to apply the pattern to your project surface.

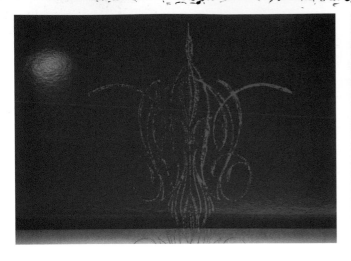

STEP 3

First, wipe the surface with a damp cloth and then degrease it. Next, tape the pattern in place. Draw a center line on the project surface and line it up to the pattern's center line. Rub the pounce bag across the pattern to transfer it to the project surface. Blow off any excess powder—too much of it will affect your striping.

STEP 4

Load the striping wheel with un-thinned enamel. Prime the tube by pushing the plunger up until you see paint peeking out of the top by the wheel. Run the wheel across a palette (the surface of an old magazine or phone book will work) to start the paint. You must do this every time you start a new line or change directions, otherwise the line will have a skip at the beginning. Start the wheel on its edge and slowly straighten up to continue the line. Finish the line by rolling the striping wheel back on its edge again. Tip: To hold the striping wheel properly, think of it as a striping brush, not as a pencil.

STEP 5

Wait until the first color has dried, then apply the second color using the same method. Use a sword striper to create the thick flairs or to turn the corners if you have trouble doing this with the striping wheel.

STEP 6

Add a highlight to the thick sections of the stripe by taking the original color and adding some white to it. You may also darken the sections using black or purple added to the original color. Load up the sword striper and slowly pull up to create a point to the line, pushing down as you start.

STEP 7

The striping wheel comes with three guides that fit in the top of the tube to help you create straight lines. The most popular is the magnetic strip. After making sure it's straight, set the guide up against the magnetic strip and work backward along the vehicle. Use your thumb to make sure the guide stays tight to the strip. The wheel will track away from the strip if you do not keep the two parallel.

You can also use a yardstick for painting short lines on nonmetallic surfaces. Either hold it or tape it in place. Another method is a body crease, which is the trickiest to keep parallel. Place a piece of tape at the end of the guide so that you don't mark the surface of the vehicle. If none of these methods work for you, you can use a tape guide (masking tape), but you cannot use the striping wheel guide for this—it cannot track along small edges like tape. Use your index finger to track along the edge of the tape, and the line will stay parallel to the tape. Practice starting and stopping the striping wheel, twisting the barrel as you go. Remember to keep the barrel perpendicular to the surface to keep the line consistent.

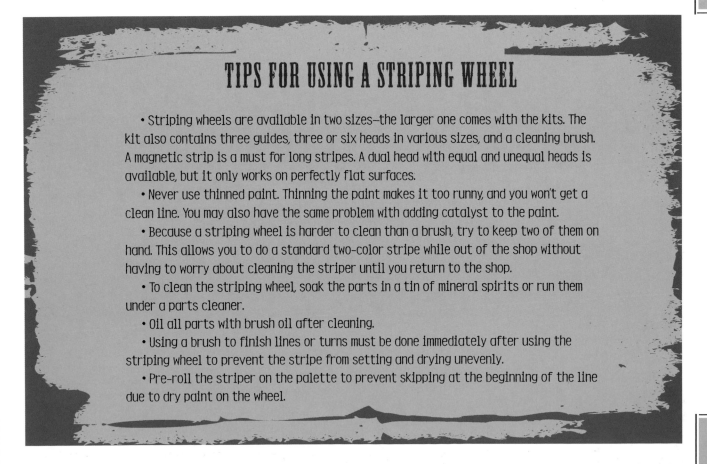

TIPS FOR USING A STRIPING WHEEL

• Striping wheels are available in two sizes—the larger one comes with the kits. The kit also contains three guides, three or six heads in various sizes, and a cleaning brush. A magnetic strip is a must for long stripes. A dual head with equal and unequal heads is available, but it only works on perfectly flat surfaces.

• Never use thinned paint. Thinning the paint makes it too runny, and you won't get a clean line. You may also have the same problem with adding catalyst to the paint.

• Because a striping wheel is harder to clean than a brush, try to keep two of them on hand. This allows you to do a standard two-color stripe while out of the shop without having to worry about cleaning the striper until you return to the shop.

• To clean the striping wheel, soak the parts in a tin of mineral spirits or run them under a parts cleaner.

• Oil all parts with brush oil after cleaning.

• Using a brush to finish lines or turns must be done immediately after using the striping wheel to prevent the stripe from setting and drying unevenly.

• Pre-roll the striper on the palette to prevent skipping at the beginning of the line due to dry paint on the wheel.

custom PT CRUISER

BY ENAMEL

Enamel was born in Iwaki City in Fukushima, Japan, in 1966. Inspired by the work of Ed "Big Daddy" Roth, Enamel began his pinstriping career in 1990. He made his U.S. debut in 1998, and since then he has been recognized as one of the world's foremost pinstripers. At the 1999 Yokohama Hot Rod Custom Show, he was named Speed King after winning the show's pinstriping race. Since then, his appearances have included the Cruising Nationals 1999–2002 in Paso Robles, California; the Rat Fink Reunion 1999; and the Tokyo Groovy 2000 and 2001. Follow along with Japanese line master Enamel as he pinstripes this PT Cruiser.

MATERIALS & EQUIPMENT

Blue, light blue lettering enamel
#000 sword striper
Reducer
Water-based greased pencil

PREP

To prepare for striping work, mix blue with reducer. Then clean the surface of the car with wax and grease remover to eliminate any dust and grime.

Next, draw your center guideline with a water-based grease pencil and palette your brush with blue.

(Enamel applies powder to his hands to help them slide over his striping surface more easily.)

STEP 1

Draw a guideline down the center of the hood.

STEP 2

Using the sword striper, lay down your center line.

STEP 3

As the line develops, work back and forth, starting with the left side of the design and then moving on to the right side.

STEP 4

Continue to build up your design, balancing your dominant hand on top of your non-dominant hand for maximum support.

STEP 5

Still using the blue, expand the design, paying close attention to symmetry and balance.

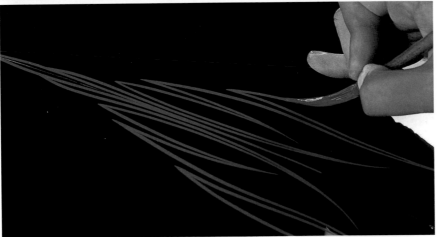

STEP 6

Complete the outside of the line.

STEP 7

Next, wrap up the blue with a long, curved line.

STEP 8

Next, use light blue, the second and final color in this design.

STEP 9

The design unfolds as you use the light blue to complete the pinstriped masterpiece.

CHAPTER
5.5

pinstriping, JAPANESE style

BY TAKAHIRO "WILDMAN" ISHII

In this how-to, Japanese pinstriper Takahiro "Wildman" Ishii brings his signature automotive art to a pair of leather pants for an incredible hot rod look. When asked what he thought was the standard that pinstripers should be judged by—speed, style, or accuracy—he said that all of those are important, but in his eyes, consistency in line stroke weight is a true measure of a striper's skill. No matter what level striper you are, though, Ishii stresses practice, practice, and more practice. Follow along with him for a chance to hone those striping skills with this very wearable example of custom culture.

MATERIALS & EQUIPMENT
Lettering enamel
Striping brushes
China marker
Airbrush

STEP 1
Start by sketching a rough draft using the china marker.

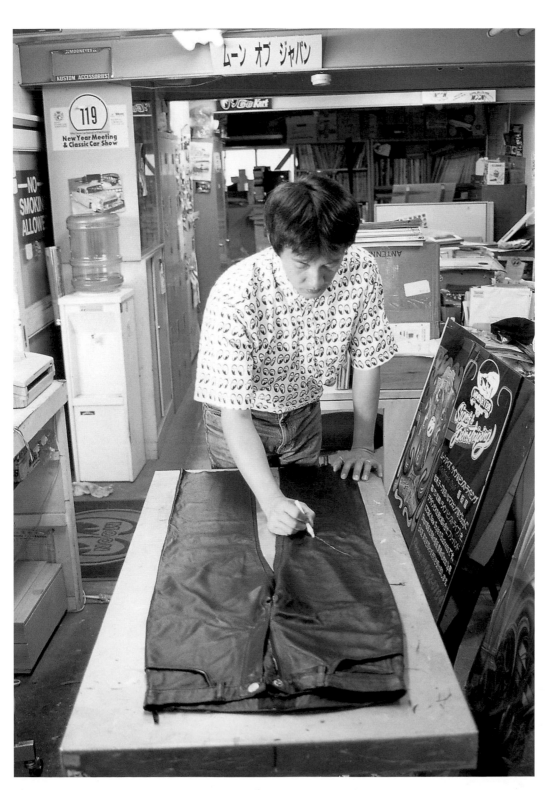

STEP 2

Draw the flames by hand
using enamel.

STEP 3

Using an airbrush, draw the familiar
brush onto the pants and begin the
flamed-out background.

STEP 4

Next, pinstripe the idea onto the
leather pants.

STEP 5

Draw a '57 Ford on one pant leg using the airbrush and pinstripe brush.

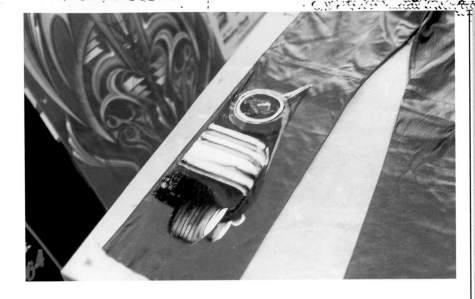

STEP 6

Stripe a spider web using the brush.

STEP 7

Here's the finished backside of the pants.

"Wildman" shows off his finished pinstriped leather pants with a decidedly custom-culture theme. This project took about two days to complete, back and front, as one side had to dry before the other side could be painted.

pinstriping a MOTORCYLE tank

BY JON KOSMOSKI

Jon Kosmoski, the founder of House of Kolor, began painting friends' helmets and motorcycle parts shortly after finishing high school. By the mid 1960s, he was manufacturing his own line of custom finishes while operating a body shop specializing in quality crash work. In 1983, after winning more than a hundred "Best Paint" awards at car shows nationwide, Jon closed the body shop to keep up with the growing demand for his paint products. That same year, he introduced his Kosmic Urethane custom paints, and his business grew explosively. By the mid 1990s, House of Kolor's sales were in the millions. Jon sold the company to the Valspar Corporation, where he remains an active consultant working on new products.

This project uses pure acrylic urethane pinstriping paint. You can use these paints without a catalyst if you're going to clear coat them. If not, use a catalyst. Because these paints are low build with high pigmentation, they're easy to level with clear coats, and they are excellent for airbrush use with reduction.

MATERIALS & EQUIPMENT
Blue, pink striping paint
#00 striping brushes
Reducer
500- or 600-grit sandpaper

STEP 1

Pulling the paint from a palette is very important—it gives you a chance to feel the paint before you begin the application. Put some of the blue on the card and then add reducer until the paint has the right consistency. Palette the paint on a hard surface. Some artists use phone books, but we don't recommend that because the paper will absorb the solvents. Use a hard glossy surface that won't absorb the solvents, but will allow you to work the paint into the hair of the brush.

STEP 2

Support one hand with the other while striping. Pulling a straight line means first working enough paint up into the heel of the brush so that you don't run out halfway down the line. Always be sure the brush remains flexible. If it's not, return to the palette and add reducer to make sure the brush is loose.

STEP 3

It's important to apply the pinstriping to a catalyzed topcoat. This tank has already been cleared, but before pinstriping, wet-sand it with 500- or 600-grit paper. Remember that when striping without a catalyst, wet-sanding the area ensures adhesion of both the pinstripe paint and the final clear coats.

STEP 4

Urethane striping enamel is easy to use—any mistakes can be easily wiped off with a little acetone on a rag.

STEP 5

When you return to the card for more paint, you can feel the tension in the paint. Add more paint or reducer as needed to create just the right consistency. You must also work some paint up into the heel of the brush, a skill that comes with practice.

STEP 6

To run a nice straight line, you need good technique and a paintbrush that carries enough paint to complete the line without having to stop and go back to the card.

STEP 7

Corners require that you lift and twist the brush or you'll get an inconsistent line. For tight turns, reload the brush to ensure adequate paint flow. Rotate the brush as you stripe the curve. If you don't rotate the brush, it will flatten out and the line will vary in width as you go around the circle.

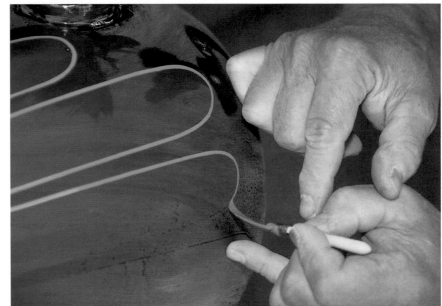

STEP 8

At the front of the tank, add some freehand striping in an abstract pattern. Before finishing, use a second color, pink, to add another dimension to the pinstripe design.

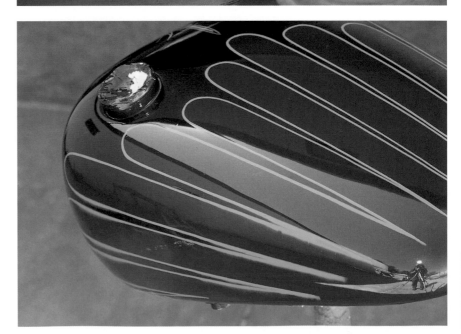

the LINE DOCTOR

BY HERB MARTINEZ

Herb Martinez has been involved with custom painting and pinstriping since he was 12 years old. Now, at age 57, his striping brush takes him around the world to shows in the United States, Europe, and Japan. Over the years, Herb has picked up pinstriping techniques from some of the top people in the business. Legendary Tommy "The Greek" was the first pro he ever saw stripe. Since then, Herb has found mentors in greats such as "Saint" John Morton, Red Lee, Steve Fineberg, Ken Tomashiro, and, perhaps his greatest influence, Cary Greenwood, who hired Herb in 1978 for Classic Vans in Fremont, California. This job permanently changed the course of his professional career.

Herb is a man who definitely gives credit where credit is due. He has a long list of major influences, but perhaps his most important laurel is that he is a past recipient of the Von Dutch pinstripe award from the Oakland Roadster show. Only a very exclusive club of stripers can lay claim to that. Watch as the "Line Doctor" shows off his incomparable striping skills in this demonstration.

MATERIALS & EQUIPMENT

Magenta, purple, blue lettering enamel
#00 sword striper
1/4-inch crepe tape
White masking paper
Blue fineline vinyl masking tape
#2 pencil
#9 pounce wheel
Chalk or pounce bag
Sea sponge

STEP 1

On this PT Cruiser, you'll use two different styles of flames: the old classic style on the hood and a modern elongated style on the sides. The elongated style is called "snake" flames, a style popularized in the San Francisco Bay area in the early 1970s.

Lay the side design using a freehand technique with 1/4-inch crepe tape. The 1/4-inch tape turns a better curve than thicker tapes; it lays flat and gives a good surface to mask up to.

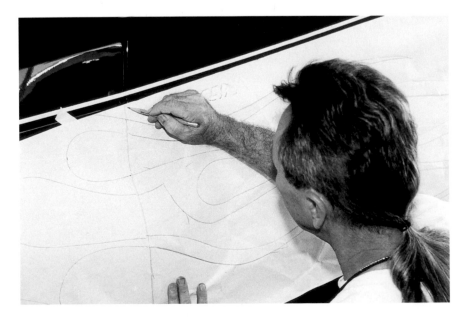

STEP 2

After you lay out the flames on one side, cover up the design with white masking paper. This allows you to trace the design to match the other side. Using a #2 pencil, trace the existing flames by running the pencil on the edge of the tape under the paper.

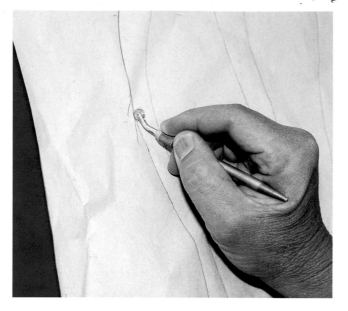

STEP 3

With the tracing finished, lay the paper on a layout
board (you can use a table with a felt cover). Then take
the #9 pounce wheel and start pouncing the pattern. This
wheel punches small holes along the pencil line to help
transfer the design to the other side of the PT later.

STEP 4

Position the pounced paper on the opposite side of the
PT. Using a chalk (or pounce) bag, pat the surface until
all the holes in the pounced pattern have been chalked.
Then carefully lift the paper to make sure the pounce
transferred well enough to trace with your tape.

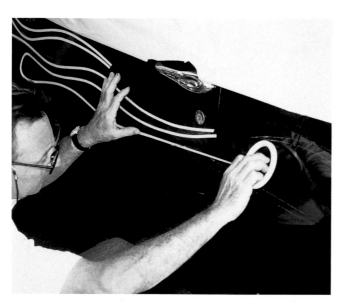

STEP 5

A good rule of thumb: Don't completely remove the
pattern right away. Lift it above the design—that way if
something happens to the chalk lines, you can always
drop the pattern back into place. Using the same crepe
tape, trace the design left by the chalk. This gives you
the exact design on both sides.

STEP 6

After making sure the tape is laid out correctly, use
some compressed air and a tack rag to erase any leftover
chalk dust. This is also a good time to pull off the
pattern and wipe off any dust on the rest of the PT
Cruiser that may hinder your painting.

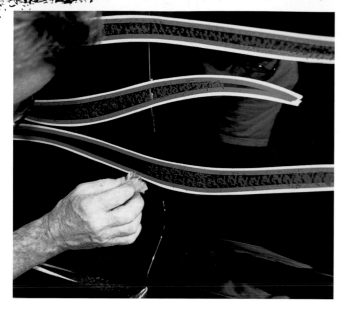

STEP 7

Lay in some blue fineline vinyl masking tape about 1/8 inch inside the crepe tape. This gives you a natural border on the inside of the flame layout for your sponge work. Using magenta, create a sponge effect with a piece of sea sponge, dabbing the paint in a gradated pattern, almost like an airbrushed fade, but coarser.

STEP 8

After finishing with the magenta, go to the purple and continue the sponging to create a two-color texture.

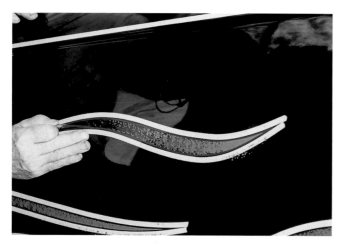

STEP 9

With the sponging finished, carefully remove the tape, leaving your 1/8-inch gap to stripe in. The masking and gap not only make the striping easier and faster, but since the pinstripe fills in the gap, you have less overall edge, allowing the flames to last longer. Lay out the pinstripe using blue and a #00 sword striper.

STEP 10

Make sure to pull your tape before it completely dries— this allows the paint to fold over slightly, and gives a more rounded line, without that nasty edge.

Sponged flames make a very handy "upsell"—a special upgrade to the job that allows you to charge a little more. A job this size without sponging goes for about $350, but by adding this simple technique, you can charge up to $500.

Before attempting this design on a vehicle, try practicing it on some old fenders. This is much cheaper than cleaning your mishaps off a customer's car and possibly ruining the base paint in the process. In this industry, some of the simplest designs and techniques can make you the most money if performed and promoted correctly.

custom PAINTING
a guitar body

BY PAUL QUINN

Recently, a body shop owner and top-notch guitarist requested a special job for him. He wanted to pay tribute to his late sister by naming and then decorating one of his guitars in her honor. Follow along as we combine lettering and striping techniques to make this guitar a truly unique showpiece.

MATERIALS & EQUIPMENT

Metallic gold, purple, violet, blue, green lettering enamel
Powdered pearls
#0 striping brush
#2 scrolling script brush
#4 extended lettering quill
Solvent
Blue fineline vinyl masking tape
White graphite pencil
Hardener
Reducer
Clear coat
Plastic supermarket bag or plastic wrap

CUSTOM PAINTING A GUITAR BODY

5.8

STEP 1

It's best to start with a guitar that is freshly painted, clear coated, and wet-sanded flat—all ready to rock and roll!

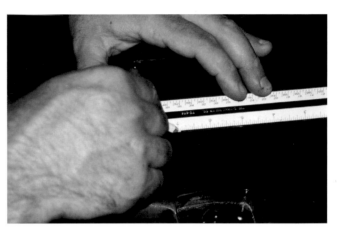

STEP 2

After wiping down the guitar with a wax and grease remover, begin laying out some simple guidelines with a white graphite pencil for spacing purposes. The graphite pencil is water-soluble, so you can easily remove these lines before applying the final clear coat.

STEP 3

Next, lay the baseline and capline for the lettering of the name, "Nadine." Following the curves of the guitar, draw the lettering using the graphite pencil.

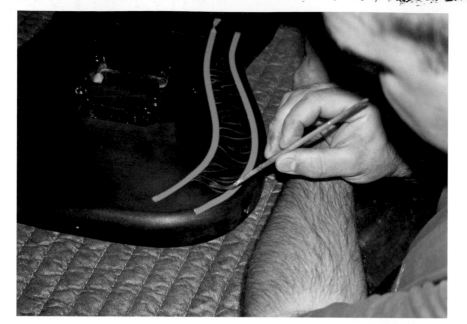

STEP 4

Using an extended lettering quill, letter "Nadine" (or the name of your favorite girl or boy) using clear coat with a small amount of powdered pearl mixed in. Use reducers here and, because the art will be clear coated with a urethane, add hardener, at about 10 percent by volume. Note the sparkle the pearl adds to the black base.

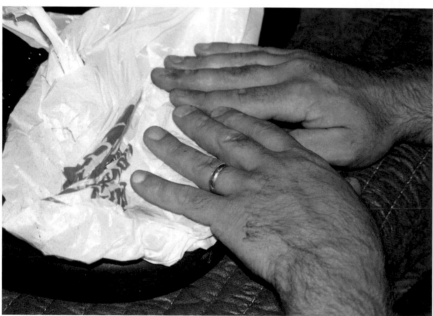

STEP 5

Immediately upon completing the lettering, "bag" the pearl using the plastic bag. You could also use plastic wrap for this technique. The finished look is a marblized "Nadine."

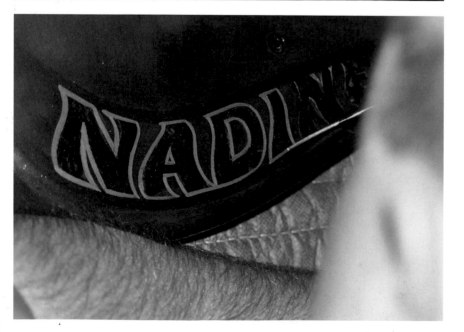

STEP 6

After removing the blue fineline vinyl tape, mix some metallic gold with purple to achieve a metallic burnt orange. Add hardener and reducer and outline "Nadine" using a #2 scrolling script brush.

STEP 7

Now that the lettering is done, begin striping a music note, which will be the central point of the striping.

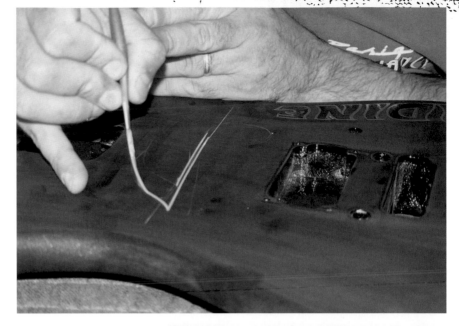

STEP 8

For the striping, use the #0 striping brush. The color is a mix of violet and purple. Use your hands to support the brush.

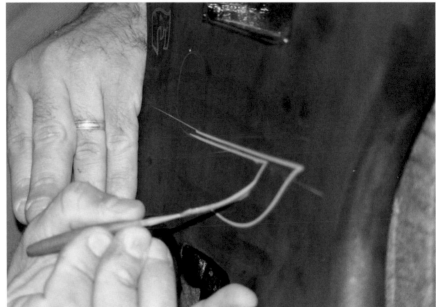

STEP 9

The next color is blue, with a drop or two of purple to warm it up a little.

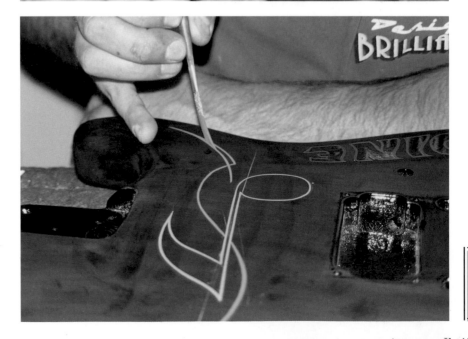

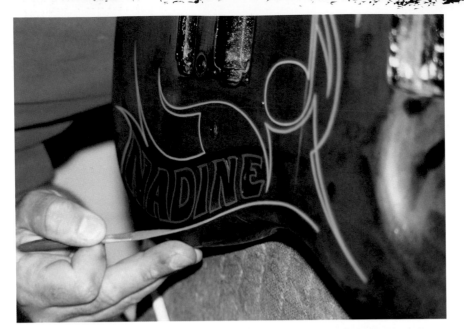

STEP 10

Because the guitar's shape differs
from side to side, go with an
asymmetrical design. This allows
you to work randomly with the body
of the guitar. The goal is to
achieve balance both in color and
weight.

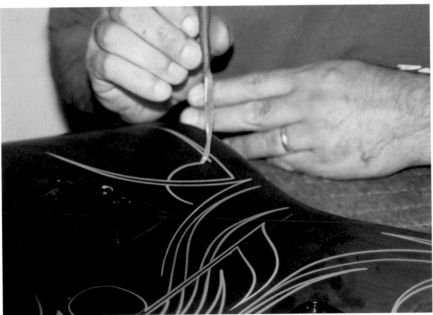

STEP 11

Build upon the design using green.
Note how the brush is at a 90-
degree angle to the surface and is
on its tip for proper execution of
the tight curve.

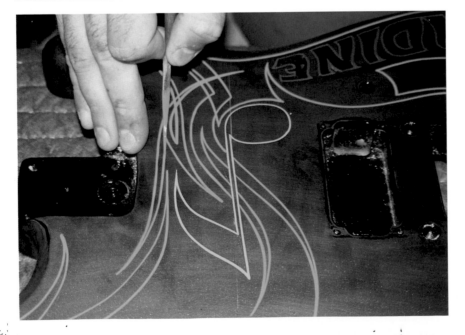

STEP 12

Continue with the green using a
more traditional thumb and
forefinger hold for more lengthy
subtle curves.

STEP 13

Changing to a mix of purple with
some violet (a darker mix than the
music note), continue to build upon
the design. Because of the size and
shape of the guitar, you can easily
move around and stripe from all
sides. (This is a welcome change
after working in tight spots on
cars and motorcycles.)

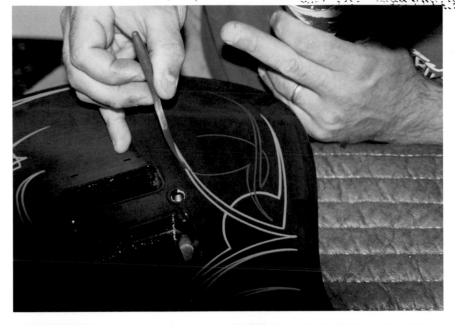

STEP 14

Adding a little more violet to the
mix, build up the design with some
teardrop-shaped accent lines.

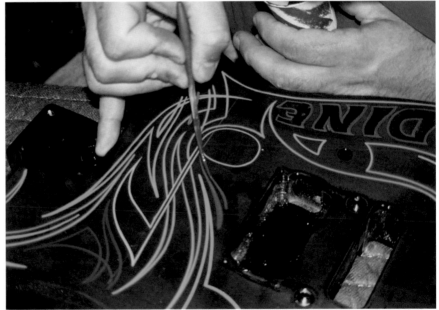

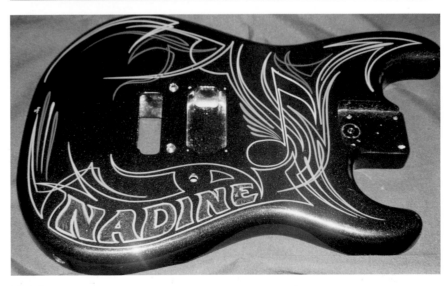

All done! Leave the guitar to dry overnight, clear coat it, wet-sand it, and polish it to a glass-like finish.

a pinstriped TIKI

BY VON FRANCO

Back in 1963, 13-year-old Frank Costanza rode his bike to the local auto show to see Rat Fink painting legend Ed "Big Daddy" Roth. After he showed Roth one of his own T-shirt designs (mostly done with a felt-tip marker and rattle cans), Roth took the shirt and gave the boy a piece of paper with one word scribbled on it. Roth kept the shirt, saying it was the price for the secret, and that single word was all Frank needed to know.

The word was "Paasche," and three decades and countless Paasche airbrushes later, Frank, now known in the industry as Von Franco, still lives the custom-culture lifestyle with a vengeance. Though most of Von Franco's work is now on canvas instead of T-shirts, his Roth-influenced style is still apparent. Merging the abstract art styles of Robert Williams, Ed Newton, and Basil Wolverton with the automotive pinstriping designs of Von Dutch, Ed Roth, and Larry Watson, Franco has created a synthesized art form that is as unique as any of his mentors' work.

Formerly a member of the Lucky Devils car club of Southern California, Von Franco recently joined the infamous Beatniks car club. Aside from their love of the color purple, the Beatniks are also known for the large number of custom-culture artists who are members in good standing—Dennis McPhail, Jack Rudy, Daddy-O, and Rob Fortier, to mention just a few.

At first glance, Von Franco's work appears to be a fusion of 1950s advertising art blended with the classic imagery of 1940s and 1950s "B" movie posters. This retro style is not only timeless among the custom kar crowd, but it is also making a name for itself in art galleries and among private collectors.

Get your brushes and join Von Franco for the creation of a quintessential custom-culture design, a pinstriped Tiki.

MATERIALS & EQUIPMENT
Lettering enamel
Striping brushes
Graphite pencil
Plastic cups
Motor oil
Low-temp reducer

STEP 1
Before striping, sketch out the concept of your design.

STEP 2
Using a graphite pencil, sketch out the masterpiece for striping on your surface.

STEP 3

Use a clean set of cups to mix your custom blend of reducers. Any contaminants may cause extremely dangerous reactions.

STEP 4

For flow, use a little motor oil.

STEP 5

One of the hardest things to do when striping is to actually get started, so you might want to add a little starter fluid.

STEP 6

Franco likes this stuff because of the retro-logo on the can. He hasn't quite figured out what's in it yet, but it goes in anyway.

STEP 7

Use some reducer, which helps the striping flow better and stay wet longer for better line consistency.

STEP 8

With the reducer, if you lose the lid, you don't have to worry—the paint makes one for you. Just take out your pocketknife and peel off the top skin.

STEP 9

Trim the edges to make the brush stripe just right.

STEP 10

Notice the proper squeegee technique when paletting the brush. This allows complete absorption of lead into the cuticle.

STEP 11

A good hand position is important. Using one hand as a guide and the other hand to steady yourself, you can follow your sketch with nice clean even strokes. If you properly palette your brush, you can make the majority of these lines without having to re-palette.

STEP 12

Unlike a pen and ink design, the pinstripe design has a nice contoured shape. Starting and ending with a point, these lines are what give the design its character. Of course, knowing how to pull them is also beneficial.

STEP 13

Although you sketched this design in advance, don't be afraid to create designs as you stripe. When something in the design catches your eye, work with it to "bring it out."

STEP 14

Near the end of the design, add teeth and a few extra lines that were not in the original sketch. A good sketch is a great way to start the design process, but it should not end there—you should always modify your design, adding or subtracting from it throughout the creation process.

STEP 15

Here's the completed design in all its Tiki glory! Because this design was done with reducer, you need to remember that the paint will remain wet for at least a few hours.

STEP 16

Adding some turquoise to the yellow palette, make a nice dirty lime green to finish off the design.

STEP 17

A favorite Von Dutch striping technique: Using the classic mouth brush style, you can impress the competition, make friends, and actually stripe without reading glasses.

STEP 18

Sneezing is a common problem while using the mouth brush technique. Many would view this blob of paint as a major setback, and some may even try to fix it. You must view all your mistakes as art. Heck, even charge more for them if you can.

STEP 19

There you have it. Nice signature, cool Tiki, and even the brush becomes part of the design, after it is accidentally left there for a few hours. Jackson Pollack could not have been more proud. The only sad note is that Franco really liked that brush.

INDEX